UNDERSTANDING
PAT CONROY

UNDERSTANDING CONTEMPORARY AMERICAN LITERATURE
Matthew J. Bruccoli, Founding Editor
Linda Wagner-Martin, Series Editor

Volumes on

Edward Albee | Sherman Alexie | Nelson Algren | Paul Auster
Nicholson Baker | John Barth | Donald Barthelme | The Beats
Thomas Berger | The Black Mountain Poets | Robert Bly | T. C. Boyle
Truman Capote | Raymond Carver | Michael Chabon | Fred Chappell
Chicano Literature | Contemporary American Drama
Contemporary American Horror Fiction
Contemporary American Literary Theory
Contemporary American Science Fiction, 1926–1970
Contemporary American Science Fiction, 1970–2000
Contemporary Chicana Literature | Pat Conroy | Robert Coover | Don DeLillo
Philip K. Dick | James Dickey | E. L. Doctorow | Rita Dove | Dave Eggers
John Gardner | George Garrett | Tim Gautreaux | John Hawkes | Joseph Heller Lillian
Hellman | Beth Henley | James Leo Herlihy | David Henry Hwang
John Irving | Randall Jarrell | Charles Johnson | Diane Johnson
Adrienne Kennedy | William Kennedy | Jack Kerouac | Jamaica Kincaid
Etheridge Knight | Tony Kushner | Ursula K. Le Guin | Jonathan Lethem
Denise Levertov | Bernard Malamud | David Mamet | Bobbie Ann Mason
Colum McCann | Cormac McCarthy | Jill McCorkle | Carson McCullers
W. S. Merwin | Arthur Miller | Stephen Millhauser | Lorrie Moore
Toni Morrison's Fiction | Vladimir Nabokov | Gloria Naylor | Joyce Carol Oates
Tim O'Brien | Flannery O'Connor | Cynthia Ozick | Suzan-Lori Parks | Walker Percy
Katherine Anne Porter | Richard Powers | Reynolds Price | Annie Proulx
Thomas Pynchon | Theodore Roethke | Philip Roth | Richard Russo | May Sarton
Hubert Selby, Jr. | Mary Lee Settle | Sam Shepard | Neil Simon
Isaac Bashevis Singer | Jane Smiley | Gary Snyder | William Stafford
Robert Stone | Anne Tyler | Gerald Vizenor | Kurt Vonnegut
David Foster Wallace | Robert Penn Warren | James Welch | Eudora Welty
Edmund White | Colson Whitehead | Tennessee Williams
August Wilson | Charles Wright

UNDERSTANDING

PAT CONROY

Catherine Seltzer

The University of South Carolina Press

© 2015 University of South Carolina

Published by the University of South Carolina Press
Columbia, South Carolina 29208

www.sc.edu/uscpress

Manufactured in the United States of America

27 26 25 24 23 22 21 20 19 18 17
10 9 8 7 6 5 4 3 2

Library of Congress Cataloging-in-Publication Data
can be found at http://catalog.loc.gov/.

ISBN 978-1-61117-516-5 (cloth)
ISBN 978-1-61117-546-2 (paperback)
ISBN 978-1-61117-517-2 (ebook)

For Dave

CONTENTS

SERIES EDITOR'S PREFACE

The Understanding Contemporary American Literature series was founded by the estimable Matthew J. Bruccoli (1931–2008), who envisioned these volumes as guides or companions for students as well as good nonacademic readers, a legacy that will continue as new volumes are developed to fill in gaps among the nearly one hundred series volumes published to date and to embrace a host of new writers only now making their marks on our literature.

As Professor Bruccoli explained in his preface to the volumes he edited, because much influential contemporary literature makes special demands, "the word understanding in the titles was chosen deliberately. Many willing readers lack an adequate understanding of how contemporary literature works; that is, of what the author is attempting to express and the means by which it is conveyed." Aimed at fostering this understanding of good literature and good writers, the criticism and analysis in the series provide instruction in how to read certain contemporary writers—explicating their material, language, structures, themes, and perspectives—and facilitate a more profitable experience of the works under discussion.

In the twenty-first century Professor Bruccoli's prescience gives us an avenue to publish expert critiques of significant contemporary American writing. The series continues to map the literary landscape and to provide both instruction and enjoyment. Future volumes will seek to introduce new voices alongside canonized favorites, to chronicle the changing literature of our times, and to remain, as Professor Bruccoli conceived, contemporary in the best sense of the word.

Linda Wagner-Martin, Series Editor

ACKNOWLEDGMENTS

At the start of this project, I contacted Pat Conroy to see if he might be willing to sit for an interview. Instead he sat for multiple interviews, opened his papers to me, and, along with his gracious wife, the writer Cassandra King, invited me to their home. I am deeply grateful, and I hope this study is richer as the result of his immense generosity.

I am also indebted to friends, colleagues, and mentors who helped with this project in any number of ways, beginning, as always, with Linda Wagner-Martin, and including Patience Graybill Condellone, Kate Drowe, Jessica De-Spain, Kassie Garrison, Sharon James McGee, Maggie Schein, and Sara Miller and the rest of the (very patient) Southern Illinois University Edwardsville inter-library loan staff. I am also grateful for broader assistance I received from SIUE, including a grant that supported the initial research for this project.

Finally I'd like to express great appreciation to my family: my husband (and excellent close reader), Dave Limbrick; my son, Owen; and my daughter, Lily (who went so far as to "illustrate" many of my copies of Conroy's work in her self-appointed role as my assistant). And special thanks to my mother, Helen Seltzer, and to my father, Bob Seltzer, who served as my first reader. As has been true my entire life, I probably should have taken more of his advice.

CHAPTER 1

Understanding Pat Conroy

It is relatively naive to try to pinpoint the exact moment in which a person becomes a writer, but Pat Conroy's "origin story" is almost impossible to resist. The story, as Conroy has told it, generally runs along these lines: one summer his high school English teacher Eugene Norris took him to visit Thomas Wolfe's home in Asheville, North Carolina. For Conroy, a young man who had been immediately and fully "infected" by Wolfe's prose after being introduced to his work, the trip was an essential pilgrimage.[1] What was intended as an act of tribute became a genesis of sorts, however, when Norris took an apple from one of Wolfe's trees and handed it to Conroy, telling him, "Eat it, boy." With that bite, Conroy explains, "I was given the keys to go out and try to write."[2] This story's evocation of the tree of knowledge—and its perils—brims with suggestions of artistic and spiritual inheritance, yet Norris's explanation for offering Conroy the apple is equally as compelling: according to Conroy, he simply said, "I want you to understand there's a relationship between art and life."[3]

Conroy's work is interested in the sorts of dramatic patterns, resonant symbolisms, and shared mythologies evident in this snapshot from his initiation as a writer, but it is the larger relationship between life and art, so succinctly captured in Wolfe's apple, that ultimately guides his work. He has explained that "from the very beginning, I wrote to explain my own life to myself," and this connection between experience and literature informs all of his work in some way, regardless of genre.[4] Conroy is best known as a novelist, and he has published five novels: *The Great Santini* (1976), *The Lords of Discipline* (1980), *The Prince of Tides* (1986), *Beach Music* (1995), and *South of Broad* (2009). Interestingly, though, Conroy has published an equivalent number of books that are explicitly autobiographical; his memoirs include *The Water Is Wide* (1972), *My Losing Season* (2002), and *The Death of Santini* (2013), as well as a culinary memoir (*The Pat Conroy Cookbook,* 2004) and an intellectual memoir (*My Reading Life,* 2010).[5] Indeed this neat balance in Conroy's creative output (which is rounded out by a 1970 book of sketches and reminiscences, *The Boo*) is representative of the porous nature of art and experience in his work.

Just as William Faulkner relentlessly paced his "own postage stamp of native soil," Conroy regularly returns to the fertile ground of his own family life in his both his fiction and his autobiographical work, noting, "Only rarely have I drifted far from the bed where I was conceived."[6] Echoing Leo Tolstoy's maxim, Conroy has wryly observed, "One of the greatest gifts you can get as a writer is to be born into an unhappy family. I could not have been born into a better one. They're from Central Casting. Mom and Dad were Athena and Zeus. I don't have to look very far for melodrama. It's all right there."[7] "Zeus" was Donald N. Conroy, a Marine Corps fighter pilot whose violent and unpredictable temper rendered him an unfathomable colossus. Pat, born on October 26, 1945, was the eldest of seven children, and Don viewed his young family as he might a particularly disappointing series of recruits, regularly baiting, belittling, and beating them in his attempt to create "good soldiers."[8] Thus the Conroy children were left with a paradoxical understanding of their father: on one hand, Don Conroy was a model of American masculinity, a true hero who served in three wars. On the other, he was a terrifying and abusive husband and father, a cipher who existed as "The Great Santini," the sobriquet he borrowed from a daring aerialist as a way of communicating his almost mystical—and certainly unquestioned—power. Conroy has sardonically observed that "I never thought he could tell the real difference between a sortie against the enemy and a family picnic," and has said more plainly, "I grew up thinking my father would one day kill me."[9]

It is not surprising, then, that his father's shadow loomed over every aspect of Conroy's childhood and has extended into his understanding of himself as an author. Conroy describes his father's attacks as both unpredictable and brutal, and his interviews, essays, and autobiographical works are marked by recollections of beatings that left him both bloodied and betrayed. Moreover the enforced peripateticism of the Marine Corps ensured that the Conroy children never lived anywhere long enough to create a sense of stability to balance Don Conroy's volatility: the Conroys moved over twenty times before Pat graduated high school, a period in which he understood that "my job was to be a stranger, to know no one's name on the first day of school, to be ignorant of all history and flow and that familial sense of relationship and proportion that makes a town safe for a child."[10] This alienation from a larger community both bound Conroy more closely to his family and, ultimately, shaped his fascination with the intricacies of the "history and flow" of the larger world that, throughout his childhood, he was able to observe but rarely join in any meaningful way.

Frances "Peggy" Peek Conroy's "Athena" was an even more complex figure.[11] In many ways she served as a perfect foil to her husband: his South Side Chicago gruffness was matched by her pronounced southern graciousness; his quick Irish temper was contrasted with her quiet shrewdness; and his strength was paired with her soft beauty. Conroy has spoken and written about her extensively, noting that if his fiction is preoccupied with his father's violent bequest, as a novelist he is equally the inheritor of his mother's faith in the power of language. In his literary memoir, *My Reading Life,* Conroy writes that "my mother hungered for art, for illumination, for some path to lead her to a shining way to call her own. She lit signal fires in the hills for her son to feel and follow. I tremble with gratitude as I honor her name."[12] Elsewhere he similarly credits Peggy with nurturing his sense of ethics, noting that she read Anne Frank's *Diary of a Young Girl* to her children when they were little. As opposed to Don Conroy, whom Conroy identifies as "a racist, anti-Semitic, anti-everything," Peggy told her children that "she wanted [them] to become the kind of family that would hide Jews." This identification of bravery rooted in humanitarian rather than militaristic actions, as well as his mother's recognition of the absolute power of language, "affected my entire life," says Conroy.[13]

Yet while Peggy Conroy floats through much of Conroy's work as an ethereal, transcendent presence—particularly in her incarnation as Lillian, the beautiful and long-suffering wife of the brutish Bull Meecham (modeled closely after Don Conroy) in Conroy's autobiographical novel *The Great Santini*—he recognizes that she is a much more complex figure in reality. Even as she read to her children from *Diary of a Young Girl* and *Gone with the Wind,* both texts that serve as testaments to the power of a single voice to shape, preserve, and even subvert history, she would not let any of the children speak openly about their father's violence, and, in fact, throughout their childhood she denied its existence.[14] Conroy explains that after she had been hit by Don, Peggy "would recover and tell us that we had not seen what we had just seen. She turned us into unwitnesses of our own history."[15] Thus the Conroy children grew up in a house in which bravery and action were central tenets of an orthodox faith, yet Pat, along with his brothers and sisters, was forced into a position of passivity and silence throughout his childhood.

At the same time, however, Peggy paradoxically was giving Pat the tools he would need to restore his own testimony; she was particularly focused on her two eldest children, Pat and Carol, fostering their love of reading and their appreciation of language with the specific goal that they would one day become writers.[16] Conroy has speculated that Peggy's wish for him to become a novelist may partly have stemmed from her need to ameliorate the silences she herself had accepted in her role as a dutiful wife as well as those she felt were imposed upon her because of her limited education, a source of lasting shame for her. Conroy explained to one interviewer that "I think why Mother wanted so badly for me to be a writer—and this was part of her unconscious, something she would not be able to express—was simply because of this: She wanted me to be the voice of her family, especially her voice. And families like Mom's and mine are voiceless for centuries. And suddenly we go to college, and we read the great books of the world. And we look around and we realize our family has stories also."[17]

To serve as Peggy's voice, though, would be a nearly impossible task. On one hand she was driven by a desire to be recognized and understood, and it is interesting that while she objected to Conroy's portrait of his family in *The Great Santini* because it exposed family secrets, she also took issue with what she perceived to be Conroy's overly generous depiction of her, stating that Lillian was "a sappy, tacky, spineless creature, not the fighter you know me to be."[18] Yet, on the other hand, even as she chastised Conroy for the inauthenticity of his portrait of her, Peggy was also a person who was continually engaged in a process of tightly controlled reinvention. As Conroy has described her in interviews, essays, and, most recently, in his memoir *The Death of Santini*, Peggy had a very clear image of who she wanted to be, and she understood that even the most manufactured of personas may comfortably ossify into fact over time. With Scarlett O'Hara's model in mind, then, she reinvented her history, burnishing it so that it seemed more romantic and so that it facilitated her ability to "pass" as the modern belle she aspired to be: in her telling, her family had lost its fortune in the Civil War, a narrative that denied the Peek family's long history of poverty, and Peggy came to tell people she had "almost graduated" from Agnes Scott College, even though, in fact, she had not gone to college at all.

Moreover Peggy revised her children's histories as well: for instance she would not acknowledge her son Tom's schizophrenia nor Carol's ongoing struggles with mental illness.[19] This silence, like that she displayed in the face of Don's abuse, is consistent with almost any construction of southern ladyhood, but it also took a significant toll on the Conroy children: they found much of their own identities and experiences written out of their mother's narrative, or, as painfully, reincorporated when it suited her purpose. For example when *The Great Santini* was published, Peggy offered an "appraisal [of the novel that] was withering and remorseless," and that, as Conroy writes, "sliced away at the most tender parts of me."[20] Then, in an unanticipated reversal, she used the book as evidence of Don's bullying and abuse when she divorced him after thirty-three years of marriage, appropriating Conroy's work in support of her case. Conroy notes that "in the courtroom, Mom took the stand and testified about every act of violence I described in *The Great Santini,* even though I'd made up most of those particular scenes, culling bits and fragments from a lifetime of mistreatment to fuel the fires."[21] For Peggy Conroy, truth was an ever-shifting notion.

If it is difficult to grow up in a house shaped by such perilous domestic politics, it is equally challenging to define oneself apart from that history in adulthood; rather understandably, then, Pat Conroy's choices after graduating from high school and leaving the family home often bear the visible mark of his family's influence. Some decisions can be clearly identified as the result of coercion: for instance after his father submitted an application on his behalf without any prior discussion, Conroy attended the Citadel, a private military academy that replicated Don Conroy's brutal ethos and, accordingly, that was ill-suited to provide the sort of deep liberal arts education that Conroy craved. Other choices, however, are marked by a subtler attempt by Conroy to repair or even rewrite his damaged past. For example, immediately after he left the Citadel, he accepted a high school teaching position in Beaufort, South Carolina, the town where his family had settled in Don's final years in the Marine Corps and where Pat had spent his junior and senior years of high school. The move was a significant one for Conroy; in choosing to become a teacher, he was signaling his embrace of a model of manhood that was defined in large part by his own beloved teacher and mentor, Gene Norris, and, consequently, one that veered sharply away from that presented to him by his father. Yet at the same time, it is telling that Conroy returned to a place that was unmistakably marked by his family history rather than starting afresh in a different town. He has explained that after a lifetime of moving in support of his father's career, he was desperate for a sense of belonging, and from his earliest days, "I latched on to [Beaufort] like a barnacle."[22] Beaufort, a small coastal town rich with its own history, seemed a perfect balm to his sense of rootlessness and perhaps even offered a way to reframe his relationship to his family.

Conroy has been married three times, and it is interesting to note that his relationships with the family into which he was born and with the family he created intersect in complex and often damaging ways.[23] For instance Conroy's first marriage, to Barbara Bolling Jones,[24] ended in part because of the emotional unmooring Conroy experienced in writing about his family life in *The Great Santini,* which became a full-blown nervous breakdown as his family "exploded" in the aftermath of the novel's publication.[25] Conroy's second marriage, to Lenore Fleischer, similarly ended in divorce and another breakdown. By all accounts the marriage had been fraught from its early days, but toward its close Conroy revealed his deep anxiety about his fitness for marriage—and family life in general—to an interviewer, saying, "What got left out of my childhood is that no one taught me how to love. Love in my family came with fists. The human touch was something to be feared. . . . I've never known how to love the women in my life, my children, my brothers and sisters, my friends. I can fake it—I can pretend and make believe—but I don't have a clue about what love is about."[26] Conroy characterizes his third marriage, to the novelist Cassandra King, as filled with "harmony and peace and joy," and as in any strong marriage, there may be endless reasons for its success, perhaps as inexplicable as a magical alchemy.[27] It seems worth noting, though, that their courtship was cemented during the period of Don Conroy's final illness and death. Don had undergone a dramatic transformation after coming to terms with the portrait Pat had painted in *The Great Santini*, and the two men had developed a close— if at times uneasy—relationship over the intervening decades. The final stages of Don Conroy's life triggered a period of self-reflection for Pat, and it seems significant that he and Sandra were married within weeks of Conroy's entry into "a new, fatherless world."[28]

Given its enormous impact, then, perhaps it is not surprising that Conroy would return to his family's history repeatedly in his work. With a few notable exceptions, his protagonists must come to terms with a mercurial and violent father, one whose often irrational cruelty is supported by a set of institutional mores, be they regional, military, or religious. As these fathers age and begin to sense the onset of their own decline, they scramble to keep their power through a sort of primal meanness, articulated concisely by Jack McCall's father in *Beach Music*, Johnson Hagood, who reveals to his son, "I look for things that'll hurt you the most, then I use them for pleasure. It's a sport I invented" (393). The mothers in Conroy's work tend to wield a less conspicuous power but are often shrewder than their husbands and thus even more dangerous. Despite a mannered, even warm, exterior, these women remain distanced and wary, engaged in a continual performance that is equal parts practiced opacity, choreographed self-revelation, and carefully aimed flattery. Finally the children in Conroy's work often develop a wry humor, a shared shorthand for making sense of their damaged childhoods. Ultimately, however, they can only provide limited comfort for one another; their fear and insecurity drive them to seek out surrogate families comprising teachers, coaches, and friends or, more dramatically, to isolate themselves further in madness and despair.

The domestic focus of Conroy's work is overlaid by a larger preoccupation with southern identity. Known for his lyrical depictions of the South Carolina lowcountry, Conroy's work is deeply interested in the South's spiritual geographies as well, and his memoirs and novels often trace the tragic consequences of a skewed understanding of southern tradition that is then inflated and taken to violent extremes. In almost all of Conroy's novels, readers encounter protagonists who are confronted with a code of honor that has been invented in the absence of a genuine chivalric model, one that is terrifying not only in its severity but also in its evident unsustainability: in Conroy's vision the contemporary South is, in many ways, a dangerous facsimile of its admittedly mythic antecedent. In *The Lords of Discipline,* for instance, the military itself becomes a de facto southern patriarch, enforcing a brand of masculine honor that is dependent upon physical and social humiliation, and that relies on old patterns of racial prejudice as a means of maintaining order. Similarly in Conroy's autobiography *My Losing Season,* as well as much of Conroy's fictional work, sports become a way of enforcing a specific and relatively unforgiving form of masculinity, as young men are tested and then effectively deemed to be successes or failures, an often permanent form of psychological branding. Conroy is also interested in religion's ability to dictate identity and, as crucially, to impose silence; his work is filled with Catholic characters who feel alienated in the still largely Protestant South, and are then doubly isolated by their inability to explore their own doubts, thoughts that, once articulated, become acts of terrifying sacrilege. Ultimately, then, Conroy's characters must come to terms with the ways that familial and cultural betrayals overlap, and in almost all of his work, the act of courage necessary for breaking with rigid social mores is often as scarring as it is liberating and as overwhelming as it is elucidatory.

As one might expect, the autobiographical impulse that drives Conroy's work complicates its public and critical reception. As a rule his readership is rabid in its enthusiasm, in part because they feel closely connected to Conroy. His longtime editor, Nan Talese, has remarked that his readers find their own experiences reflected in his portraits of family relationships and that, as a result, "they think Pat knows them and they sort of leap into his lap."[29] Conversely readers often feel they know Conroy as well. He has referred to his protagonists as his "made-up doubles and stand-ins and understudies" and, indeed, in addition to sharing many of the facts of his biography, Conroy's protagonists often resemble him personally: they tend to be liberal, quick-witted southern men who question the hierarchies that surround them even as they participate in them.[30] Moreover Conroy invites a sense of familiarity with his readers in his candid acknowledgment of his own struggles, including his ongoing battle with severe depression, which has left him suicidal at several points in his life, and an on-and-off dependence upon alcohol.[31] The writer Carolyn See expressed a common sentiment, then, when she began a review of *My Reading Life* by acknowledging, "Without seeming, I hope, too presumptuous or intrusive, I've always thought of Pat Conroy as a cousin or a brother or an uncle."[32]

Yet readers' sense of intimate connection to Conroy can also be credited to the fact that he has become the rare literary celebrity. His best-selling books and subsequent movie adaptations have given him a heightened sense of visibility as a literary figure, certainly, but Conroy's place in the popular imagination extends beyond that afforded most successful authors: for instance he has been profiled in magazines ranging from *People* and *Southern Living* to *Vanity Fair;* his family was featured in their own Thanksgiving special on CNN, *The Conroys: A Coming Together;* and the death of "the Great Santini" merited a lengthy obituary in the *New York Times.* Moreover Conroy's outspokenness, whether it be in support of his friends, in clarification of a feud, or in furthering what he has identified as an issue of social justice, forms a narrative that exists in tandem to his fiction. For instance he famously took up the cause of Shannon Faulkner, the first woman to enroll at the Citadel, serving not only as her vocal champion in her quest for admission but quietly financing her education; he lent his public support to *Atlanta Journal-Constitution* editor Bill Kovatch, who was pressured to resign after pushing a more progressive agenda for the paper, a battle that resulted in a particularly heated exchange between Conroy and the columnist Lewis Grizzard; and he vigorously defended his close friend Doug Marlette, who was accused of homophobia in his creation of a character in his novel *The Bridge* who resembled the writer Allan Gurganus. (In fact, when Marlette died unexpectedly, Conroy took this fight to the funeral, dismissing Gurganus and his supporters as "head lice" in his eulogy for Marlette.[33]) Conroy has linked these battles to his upbringing, explaining with a bemused shrug that "I am the son of a warrior," but they also contribute to a fairly extraordinary narrative of personal loyalty and political passion and have become a vital component of his public identity.[34]

While the autobiographical nature of Conroy's work and the earnestness of his public persona have endeared him to his readership, together they have made his critical reception much rockier. On one hand, his place in the contemporary canon seems undeniable: his books are regularly bestsellers, are anticipated by publishers and critics, and are widely—and generally favorably —reviewed. Yet the academy has tended to approach popular writers— especially those embraced by Hollywood—with suspicion, and more generally, it is uncomfortable with the blurring of autobiographical and fictional approaches without the benefit of a sly postmodern wink. Moreover Conroy's style often tends toward the dramatic: a characteristic critical complaint is that his "characters are unbearably glib, settings are incomparably lush, families are tragically broken, and the dysfunctions are endless."[35] Conroy acknowledges that that there is some truth in such accusations—he has written that "there are other writers who try for subtle and minimalist effects, but I don't travel with that tribe"—and has offered halfhearted apologies for his style: "I would like to write differently, but I have discovered to my astonishment and sometimes dismay, that I write the only way I can. I would choose to be Norman Mailer, if I could. I'd chose to be John Updike, Anne Tyler, or Joyce Carol Oates, but I can't. I find myself imprisoned in the sensibilities I was given."[36]

Conroy's expression of admiration for these writers is enlightening, but to understand Conroy's sense of himself as a writer more fully, it may be more helpful to consider his response to his literary forebears rather than his contemporaries, beginning most obviously with William Faulkner, arguably the most famous chronicler of the fractured southern family. Just as Flannery O'Connor identified Faulkner as the Dixie Limited bearing down on the unsuspecting mule carts that function as stand-ins for southern writers daring to work in his wake, Conroy is quick to acknowledge that "Faulkner is so much better than me. Faulkner is such an icon to me." Yet tellingly he adds, "He represents so much, but he's not my favorite writer by any means. I don't feel the passion and response I like to feel when I'm reading him. There's something cold and re-mote about Faulkner that has never touched me. . . . None of Faulkner's novels have ever changed my life."[37] Such a claim is surprising in a number of ways. It is, of course, a bold act of heresy in the South, where Faulkner remains central to almost any construction of southern literary history, and it also rejects a seemingly obvious lineage: many of Conroy's characters seem the bewildered heirs of Quentin Compson, searching for identity among perilously crumbling domestic and cultural scaffolding.

Yet Conroy's identification of Faulkner as "cold" is, in many ways, the key to his aesthetic. Conroy, in fact, often employs the metaphor of warmth to describe his experience as both a reader and a writer: most simply he explains that "I read for fire," and his descriptions of his favorite works are peppered with words such as *passion* and *heat*.[38] Similarly Conroy speaks of a "flam-mable desire" to create and explains inspiration by invoking the metaphor of a burning man, an image borrowed from an incident in which he saved a man in an explosion on the rue de Seine in Paris and thus became "a different human being from what I was ever meant to be."[39] Literature, in Conroy's vision, is meant not simply to impress its reader but to transform him or her.

In this way Conroy subscribes to a theory of the novel that is deeply rooted in a nineteenth-century Jamesian model, and he has explained that "I was born into the century in which novels lost their stories, poems their rhymes, paintings their form, and music its beauty, but that does not mean I had to like that trend or go along with it. I fight against these movements with every book I write."[40] Conroy's insistence on the primacy of narrative and his critical view of post-modern self-consciousness might be easily dismissed as curmudgeonly if they weren't so deeply informed. Conroy is a daunting student of literature, and his intellectual memoir, *My Reading Life,* functions in part as a testament to the extraordinary depth of his literary knowledge, the result of his commitment to read at least two hundred pages a day, beginning in high school.[41] Accordingly in the essays collected for the memoir, Conroy not only touches on work by ca-nonical and contemporary European and American authors, but also writes of his forays into the literatures of Latin America, India, and Israel, among others.

More often than not, though, Conroy is often linked to a tradition whose origins are found in the work of Thomas Wolfe. Conroy has remained an un-repentant Wolfephile, and in an essay aptly titled "A Love Letter to Thomas Wolfe," he writes that *Look Homeward, Angel*'s "impact on me was so visceral that I mark the reading of [it] as one of the pivotal events of my life. . . . I had entered into the home territory of what would become my literary terrain."[42] Conroy's early style was deeply imitative of Wolfe's, and Conroy wryly notes that one of his writing teachers at the Citadel "announced to my classmates that he would cheerfully shoot the teacher who had introduced me to the writing of Thomas Wolfe."[43] Yet even after Conroy developed as a writer and found his own voice, his work often exemplifies the characteristics that he had admired in those first encounters with Wolfe's work, which he sums up as "a passionate fluency and exuberant generosity of spirit."[44]

If Faulkner's project was to "tell about the South," then Wolfe was com-mitted to telling about the self, and if Faulkner is now accepted "as the Mi-chelangelo around whose achievement a cultural identity ['Southern-ness'] can be organized," in the words of southern literary scholar Michael Kreyling, then Wolfe is often the whipping boy of southern studies, regularly dismissed for what is seen as excessive lyricism.[45] Conroy, however, views the occasional chaos of Wolfe's fiction as a crucial counterweight in a Faulkner-besotted South. He explains that he is drawn to Wolfe, in short, because he "writes like a man on fire who does not have a clue how not to be on fire. . . . His art is over-done and yet I find it incomparably beautiful."[46] For Conroy, Wolfe represents a kind of literary experimentation that is rooted in an identifiable emotional experience—one that Conroy contends may be lost in the larger postmodernist project—and, as important, that he seeks to recuperate in his own work.[47]

Conroy's vocal admiration of Wolfe also functions as an indictment of a lit-erary establishment that has not always rewarded Wolfe's—or Conroy's—work.

For instance in "A Love Letter to Thomas Wolfe," he writes, "Critics who do not like Wolfe often despise him, and his very name can induce nausea among the best of them. That is all right. They are just critics, and he is Thomas Wolfe."[48] Similarly Conroy's defense of Margaret Mitchell's *Gone with the Wind* is framed by a recognition of the novel's status as "popular fiction," a subgenre distinct from "literature." In an essay written for the novel's sixtieth anniversary, Conroy notes that "because its readers have held it in such high esteem, it has cheapened the book's reputation as a work of art." Yet he argues that despite its tendency toward melodrama and its formal flaws, *Gone with the Wind* "works because it possesses the inexpressible magic where the art of pure storytelling rises above its ancient use and succeeds in explaining to a whole nation how it came to be this way."[49] In both of these essays, Conroy calls critics out for what he sees as a reflexive cultural snobbishness, an attitude that has unsettled Wolfe's and Mitchell's place in the canon as well as his own. In challenging accepted—and perhaps faddish—markers of what determines the value of a work of literature, Conroy both emphasizes his own belief in the value of narrative fiction and takes a defiant stance against critics whom he sees as hewing to an overly narrow set of standards.

Indeed Conroy has refused to participate in a system of literary criticism he views as unnecessarily vicious. In *The Death of Santini,* he writes that "I've held [critics] in high contempt since my earliest days as a writer because their work seems pinched and sullen and paramecium-souled," and in addition to making a commitment not to read reviews of his own work, he has adopted a policy of not reviewing others' books, declaring, "No writer has suffered over morning coffee because of the savagery of my review of his or her latest book, and no one ever will."[50] Conroy has also regularly explained that he has sought to distance himself from other writers, explaining that "some American writers are meaner than serial killers," and as a result, "I distrusted the breed and made a vow to avoid them for the rest of my life. Though I've made some great friends among writers, I've stayed away from most of them and it's made for a better and more productive life."[51] Such claims certainly reflect a genuine suspicion of the larger literary community, but they are balanced with Conroy's deep and rewarding connections within that community as well. His relationships with his editors—among them Jonathan Galassi, now president and publisher at Farrar, Straus and Giroux, and later Nan Talese, the esteemed Doubleday editor—have been overwhelmingly positive; many of Conroy's closest friends (and indeed, his wife, Cassandra King) are novelists and poets, and his letters bear witness to the fact that they have shared drafts of their work with one another. Moreover Conroy is dedicated to helping other authors; citing the generosity he was shown early in his own career, he regularly provides blurbs for the books of many new and established writers and has written introductions for a broad variety of books.[52]

After the publication of *The Death of Santini,* a book that explicitly identifies itself as the last chapter in the family saga that has served as his central preoccupation, Conroy finds himself at a crossroads. He has said that he has "at least three novels" in mind, a backlog caused in part by a series of health issues in recent years, including the development of a debilitating writer's cramp, the same disorder that struck Henry James later in his career.[53] (This diagnosis was especially alarming because Conroy writes only in longhand, a consequence of his father's refusal to allow him to take typing classes.) Before he returns to the novel, however, Conroy is experimenting with a number of different projects: he is currently working on a young adult novel, and he recently expressed an interest in writing about the significance of film in his life.[54] Conroy has also accepted a role as the editor at large for Story River Books, an imprint of the University of South Carolina Press, and has been surprised at the deep pleasure he has found in discovering and editing other writers' work.[55] As he approaches age seventy, then, he has reached a point in his career in which he is both firmly established in the public imagination and open to new directions.

CHAPTER 2

The Water Is Wide

Pat Conroy's first book, *The Boo* (1970), is a self-published tribute to Lt. Col. Thomas Nugent Courvoisie, the assistant commandant of the cadets in the years that Conroy was at the Citadel. The Boo, as Courvoisie was known, was recognized as a strict and demanding taskmaster, even among a faculty famed for these qualities, but he was also a fair and understanding man who served as a much-needed human touchstone for Conroy and his fellow cadets. Conroy was outraged by the Boo's relegation to a supply officer in 1968, and his book, which is a pastiche of reminiscences, sketches, and miscellanea from the Boo's tenure at the Citadel, serves as both a glimpse into cadet culture and, ultimately, a heartfelt condemnation of Courvoisie's treatment by Citadel administrators. *The Boo* is perhaps most significant, though, in that it marks the origin of Conroy's understanding of himself as a writer, and while it is an often "artless" book, in Conroy's own word, many of the qualities and themes that define his mature work are evident in their nascent form here.[1]

Most obvious, of course, is Conroy's impulse to expose and explore a perceived moral wrong. Reconsidering the book in his 1981 introduction, Conroy credits it with a "callow idealism and iridescent earnestness."[2] Buried within this seemingly wry dismissal, however, is his recognition of the ways in which his work is stamped by the desire to explore social injustices, particularly those of ossified institutions such as the Citadel or, more broadly, the South. More specifically Conroy's work tends to be preoccupied with the tension between an exaggerated vision of manhood, which in the case of *The Boo* is enacted by the cadets and the administration, and a quieter, more stoic construction of masculinity. Finally, even in its inherent unevenness, *The Boo* marks the emergence of Conroy's unique voice, one in which humor, outrage, and a celebration of language coexist easily on the page.

The Water Is Wide (1972), Conroy's memoir of his year teaching on South Carolina's Daufuskie Island, followed *The Boo* by just two years, but it represents a fuller articulation of the themes at the heart of *The Boo* and an expanded confidence in Conroy's prose. The books are linked in their sense of outrage—Conroy wrote *The Boo* while teaching on the island, and surely his frustrations with two often self-serving educational institutions, the Citadel and the Beaufort County School Board, must have fed one another at points—but *The Water Is Wide* stands alone as an engaging account of teaching in relative isolation on a long-neglected coastal island and a thoughtful examination of race and education in the civil rights era. And if the earnestness of *The Boo* manifests itself a bit too fully, *The Water Is Wide* adopts a wholly self-conscious view of youthful idealism. The book is not only an examination of the social injustices that have left Daufuskie—identified as Yamacraw in the book— economically, educationally, and culturally impoverished, but also a relentless examination of Conroy's own motivations for effecting change on the island and in the larger culture of the South. In his simultaneous sympathy for and critique of his (barely) younger self, then, *The Water Is Wide* functions not only as a bildungsroman of a committed teacher and his otherwise disenfranchised students, but also as a complex, if compact, look at the close of the civil rights era vis-à-vis the improbably anachronistic Yamacraw.

The structure of *The Water Is Wide* is defined by the chronological arc that begins when Conroy is hired to teach in Yamacraw's two-room schoolhouse and ends when he is unceremoniously fired after calling attention to what he characterizes as "the intellectual decimation" of the island's children by an unresponsive school system (191). Within this broader structure, though, there is a fair amount of fluidity: the year unfolds not according to a strict chronology but rather through a series of vignettes that comprise two primary narrative threads, the first of which is defined by Conroy's awareness of his students' lack of academic preparedness and his subsequent attempts to provide them with a meaningful education, and the second, which is focused on Conroy's increasing frustration with an educational system that is unequipped, or perhaps unwilling, to remedy the serious inequities he witnesses on the island. *The Water Is Wide,* then, is driven by this juxtaposition of the intimate world circumscribed by the island—and more specifically Conroy's classroom—and the world of the larger South. Ultimately he finds himself at the nexus of these two seemingly incompatible worlds, simultaneously invested in both and at home in neither.

In the memoir's opening pages, Conroy acknowledges that in many ways he had sought out just this sort of conflict. After moving to the sleepy South Carolina town of Beaufort in high school, he explains that he quickly adapted to the southern orthodoxies that defined the community, relishing the sense of security and stability the town offered him after a childhood of moving from one military base to another. He recalls that Beaufort "was a place of hushed, fragrant gardens, silent streets, and large antebellum houses. My father flew jets in its skies and I went to the local segregated high school, courted the daughter of the Baptist minister, and tried to master the fast break and the quick jump shot" (8). Yet the romantic simplicity Conroy assigns to Beaufort is challenged as the civil rights movement takes hold, and when he accepts a teaching position at his old high school after his graduation from the Citadel, Conroy finds himself navigating racial issues that had previously been invisible to him and, not surprisingly, reevaluating his own role in the racist legacy of the South. As he struggles to teach his students lessons of tolerance, he must confront his own childhood innocence and ignorance, and the early pages of *The Water Is Wide* exhibit the hallmark characteristics of what southern scholar Fred Hobson has termed "the white southern racial conversion narrative."[3] Conroy explains that "my neck has lightened several shades since former times, or at least I like to think it has" (6), and he engages in the confessionary practice of recounting the sins of his youth. As an adult Conroy is not simply an idealist but also a penitent, and thus while he had initially hoped to move from his high school teaching position to one with the Peace Corps, when that opportunity fails to materialize, it seems perfectly fitting that Conroy instead would take a job on Yamacraw. The island functions in his fantasies not only as "a place to absorb my wildest do-gooding tendency," as he notes, but as a space where he might work to right the racial injustices with which he is achingly familiar (23).

It is a minor irony, then, that when Conroy arrives on Yamacraw, he discovers that many of the island's daily realities mirror those he might have encountered in a Peace Corps post: its roads are traveled by ox-drawn carts as well as cars; in-home plumbing is a rarity; there is no widely available phone service; and no bridge connects the island to the mainland. Yet despite this physical, economic, and cultural isolation, there is also something troubling in an identification of the island as foreign, a practice that is typified by Mrs. Brown, the other teacher in the island's two-room schoolhouse, who greets Conroy by welcoming him "overseas" and explains to him that "I'm a missionary over here helping these poor people" (21). One might imagine that this characterization of the island as an exotic, primitive place in need of salvation might appeal to Conroy, who sardonically notes that in filling out his Peace Corps application he "had a tough time deciding whether [he] wanted to save Africa or Asia," but he instinctively balks at Mrs. Brown's casual evocation of a postcolonial rhetoric (15). While they literally may be overseas in that they have had to travel by boat to reach the island, and while Yamacraw's widespread poverty is disorienting, in fact the island is distinctly American, functioning as a palimpsest of a complex sociopolitical reality that ranges from the plantation era to the post–Jim Crow South. The foreignness that Mrs. Brown and others assign to Yamacraw belies the fact that the island is a remarkably cogent, if unexpected, microcosm of the American South.

Conroy recognizes the island's deep ties to southern history more fully when he observes the interaction between Mrs. Brown, who is African American, and Ezra Bennington, the white deputy superintendent who oversees the school on Yamacraw. Even in their first encounter, Conroy notes that the two engage in a dialogue that might have been ripped from a script written in an earlier century: Bennington, he observes, seems perfectly cast as "the venerable, hoary-maned administrator who tended his district with the same care and paternalism the master once rendered to his plantation. As I watched him perform his classroom routine, I also observed Mrs. Brown's reaction, a black teacher who nodded her head in agreement every time he opened his mouth to utter some memorable profundity" (22). Bennington comfortably inhabits his avuncular role, telling Conroy with great satisfaction, "I've always been able to get along with colored people. They've always loved me" (23). Mrs. Brown, on the other hand, is quick to distance herself from the islanders, making it clear to Conroy in their first meeting that she is not from Yamacraw and, indeed, that she holds the black islanders in contempt, explaining matter-of-factly to Conroy that "these people don't want to better themselves" (23).

Her faith, then, rests wholly with Bennington, and she explains with genuine earnestness that "Mr. Bennington is the only one who understands the problems of Yamacraw Island. He knows what's wrong . . . and he knows what to do about them" (21). If Conroy has come to Yamacraw brimming with a passion fueled by civil rights progressivism, he finds himself transported to an earlier South, one that is deeply dependent upon a romanticized notion of benevolent paternalism and that is skeptical, at best, of black agency. Bennington, of course, does not know "what's wrong" nor "what to do about them," a phrase that unconsciously equates the island's problems and the students themselves, but his position as a white male on the school board and his posture of sympathetic, if largely passive, consternation over the island's educational deficits are reflective of the white South's recognition of, yet continued unwillingness to challenge, the hegemonies that have long defined it.

If Bennington represents a sensibility grounded in nineteenth-century notions of chivalry, Ted Stone is emblematic of a much fiercer and more vitriolic understanding of race in the contemporary South. Stone is one of a handful of whites who live on Yamacraw, and he immediately becomes vital to Conroy in that he controls the dock and oversees all of the government jeeps. It is clear to Conroy, however, that Stone is a classic xenophobe, spouting hate-fueled assessments of the black islanders as well as the hippies and communists he fears are ruining the country. Moreover Stone benefits from a form of white privilege that is surprisingly antebellum in nature: for example the county built a small schoolhouse and hired a teacher so that the Stones' son, George, "wouldn't have to go to school with the coloreds," as Stone explains (70).[4]

Yet it is interesting that while Conroy depicts Bennington's insouciant paternalism and Stone's rabid sense of racial entitlement with a deeply critical eye, he also acknowledges an unexpected admiration for them. Even as he writes that Ezra "would look good dressed in a white linen suit, rocking on a high verandah, shouting orders to Negroes working in the garden below him," Conroy also identifies him as "Everyman's grandfather" and notes that "it is impossible to dislike men like Ezra. I have met a hundred of them in my life and, despite myself, have liked every one of them" (17). Similarly while he is always wary in Stone's presence, Conroy acknowledges with some appreciation that he is "a fascinating raconteur" (71) and "the quintessential outdoorsman. . . . He could plow a field, milk a cow, gut a hog, cook a trout, clean a rifle—all the things that made us such complete opposites" (69). Despite his disgust for much of what they believe, Conroy understands that it is impossible to excise the Benningtons and the Stones of the world from southern history, and it is disingenuous not to recognize his personal understanding of the values that they hold. In this way Conroy wavers between the firebrand liberalism broadly associated with the late 1960s and a variety of southern liberalism most famously represented by Atticus Finch, the even-tempered lawyer at the heart of *To Kill a Mockingbird,* Harper Lee's seminal novel about race in the South, published a dozen years earlier. Finch famously demands that his children see racists as distinct from their racism, arguing that the townspeople who seek the conviction of a black man for a crime he clearly did not commit are flawed rather than inherently evil. Unlike the eternally stoic Finch, Conroy admits he can be "self-righteous, angry, undiplomatic, unapologetic, and flaming," and while in *To Kill a Mockingbird* Finch ultimately respects judicial etiquette and quietly accepts a deeply unjust guilty verdict in the novel's central court case, in *The Water Is Wide* Conroy wages a full-on war against those he sees as responsible for perpetuating institutionalized racism, ultimately at the expense of his teaching position (190). Yet, like Finch, Conroy continually suggests that racism can be a complex and confounding thing, a component of identity rather than all-defining.

Perhaps the most profound example of this might be seen in Conroy's relationship with Zeke Skimberry, the white maintenance worker assigned by the county to assist him in his at first weekly and then daily commutes from the mainland to the island. This often perilous crossing becomes one of the central symbols of the memoir, a physical reminder both of the dramatic chasm that exists between the mainland and Yamacraw and of the intellectual and spiritual challenges that Conroy continually faces in bridging these worlds.[5] Zeke and his wife, Ida, however, serve to complicate the relatively straightforward binaries suggested in the image of the two clearly defined banks of the river through their own unconscious refusal to cede to stereotypes. For instance Conroy reports that both Zeke and Ida "mouthed the regional prejudices against blacks constantly, and believed implicitly in almost every stereotype ever concocted against blacks in the South. Yet every black man or woman I brought to their house was invited inside, offered coffee, and treated with dignity and warmth. Later, Ida would tell me, 'That was sure a nice nigger man you brought here this morning. I hope you bring him back again real soon'" (80–81). Conroy is perplexed by this profound idiosyncrasy, and he explains that he is jarred every time the Skimberrys use racist language casually or repeat discriminatory ideologies unthinkingly. Yet he is also moved by their continued generosity and unguarded honesty, and he states that he "came to love the Skimberrys devotedly" (78). On a most basic level, Zeke and Ida Skimberry cloud the rigid distinctions of good versus evil and broadmindedness versus racism. As they put Conroy in the water each morning and take his boat out each evening, the Skimberrys function as a reminder that the river is not an inviolable boundary but rather a living, fluid entity, one that suggests that an understanding of race in the South cannot be reduced to a simple formula.

As murky as the term *racist* may be, though, *The Water Is Wide* demonstrates that the consequences of institutionalized racism in the South are all too clear, and Conroy needs little time on the island to determine that his students are the collective victims of an appallingly indifferent system. By the end of the first week teaching a class that includes the eighteen children who are identified as belonging in the fifth through the eighth grades, Conroy has assembled a list of deficiencies that is both startling and heartbreaking:

> Seven of my students could not recite the alphabet. Three children could not spell their names. Eighteen children thought Savannah, Georgia was the largest city in the world. Savannah was the only city any of the kids could name. Eighteen children had never seen a hill—eighteen children had never heard the words *integration* and *segregation*. Four children could not add two plus two. Eighteen children did not know we were fighting a war in Southeast Asia. Of course, eighteen children never had heard of Asia. One child was positive that John Kennedy was the first President of the United States. Seventeen children agreed with that child. Eighteen children concurred with the pre-Copernican Theory that the earth was the center of

the universe. Two children did not know how old they were. Five children did not know their birth dates. Four children could not count to ten. (36–37)

Conroy's outrage is undeniable, and he is bewildered as he considers how he might begin to teach the children outside of the formulaic, and clearly ineffectual, strategies advocated by the school board. Moreover his task is further complicated by the fact that he has difficulty understanding his students' Gullah dialect, an obscure African and English patois, and they often cannot understand his accent, either.[6] Ultimately he forges on, using one student as a translator, and he adopts a series of unconventional pedagogical approaches designed to engage the kids in any way possible, including taping them and allowing them hear their own voices, telling them outrageous stories and inviting them to correct him, and engaging in what he calls "the pep-rally method of education" (57), an absurdist combination of trivia contest and call-and-response performance.

As Conroy details his teaching strategies, though, it becomes clear that there is one central fact that he wants all of his students to understand: there is a much larger world outside of Yamacraw. Almost all of his lessons are designed to ensure they understand that as isolated as they may be, there exists a vast richness of human experience beyond the island's shores. This is conveyed on a basic level, for instance in Conroy's decision to listen to the morning news on the radio, pointing to each place the reporter mentions on a world map that hangs in the classroom. In this exercise he is literally introducing the children to a wider geography. Even beyond this, though, he is imitating the approach of his high school English teacher and mentor, Gene Norris, who had similarly prodded Beaufort students who had grown comfortable in provincial attitudes. As Conroy recalls in *The Water Is Wide*, Norris would have his students read the *New York Times* in place of the local paper, for instance, and assigned *The Catcher in the Rye* "before the town could mobilize its committees of repression" (94). In doing so Norris asked his students to hear voices beyond those that rang loudest in Beaufort, and, perhaps, to recognize echoes of their own thoughts in this larger world. Conroy specifically recounts a time that Norris played a recording of "We Shall Overcome" for a group of students and recalls his own deep sense of shame as he heard the song. The experience did not trigger an immediate racial epiphany for Conroy, but he remembered it for years and writes that in that moment "the journey at least had a beginning, a point of embarkation" (95). Thus in listening to radio broadcasts of the morning news or in inviting a wide array of guest speakers to Yamacraw, Conroy demonstrates a similar belief that exposure to other places and voices will allow ideas to germinate in his students, just as they had taken root in him.

Moreover Conroy becomes determined that his students literally enter the larger world he is presenting to them. During his year on Yamacraw, he arranges two trips for his students, the first to Port Royal, a small town on the mainland, for an overnight Halloween celebration and the second to Washington, D.C. While the trip to D.C. is arguably more significant—the city is farther away, the trip is longer, the touristic experiences are more diverse—in many ways the trip to Port Royal is more momentous: all of the children are leaving the island for the first time, and the backdrop of Halloween, with its sublime blend of pleasure and terror, perfectly captures the inherent drama of the experience. The trip is not without its minor disasters—one student is injured and needs stitches, the river crossing back to Yamacraw is delayed for a full day because of storms—but, overwhelmingly, the trip is an unimaginable success: the children are warmly hosted by families in the white Port Royal school where Bernie Schein, Conroy's longtime friend and fellow idealist, serves as the principal, and they return to Yamacraw with not only bags of candy and stories of costumed antics but also a sense of connection to a place and traditions unknown to them only days before. The trip is recounted at the exact midpoint of the memoir, and in many ways it operates as the heart of Conroy's narrative of his teaching experience. While he often worries that he, along with Schein in this case, might be so invested in the image of themselves as "small catalysts in the transformation of the disfigured sacramental body of the South" that they are vulnerable to being blinded by their own sense of mission, Conroy realizes that the Halloween excursion "transcended our own personal preoccupations" (146). The kids, quite simply, are thrilled by the carnivalesque experience that is American Halloween and for almost all who are involved in it, the trip is marked by moments of authentic joy and meaningful personal and cultural connections.

Not all of Conroy's attempts to reach the children are successful, of course, and while he lists his shortcomings in the classroom regularly in *The Water Is Wide,* Conroy is equally troubled by his inability to challenge some of the larger values that shape the children's sense of identity. Most specifically Conroy is distressed by the kids' unabashedly cavalier attitude toward violence. He catches them dismembering frogs, tearing wings off insects, and even shooting dogs, and he is often shocked by the brutality intrinsic to their invented playground games. Lectures on basic kindness, appeals to fair play, and even a plan to get the kids to raise a litter of the Skimberrys' puppies all end in failure. Some part of the children's attitudes can be attributed to their regular exposure to the domestic violence and drunken brawls that take place on the island, but there also exists a larger, more spectral sense of impending violence, one that is potent if generally unmentioned. Looming above all else is Vietnam, of course, which Conroy acknowledges rather obliquely when he explains that he would rather teach than "romp about the marshes of Parris Island, and emerge the product of a military system I had come to loathe," or when he talks about his marriage to Barbara Jones in the fall of his year on Yamacraw, a relationship that begins shortly after her husband is killed in action (15).[7]

Even beyond this, though, the island, so far removed from international politics, is awash in its own history of violence. In one particularly evocative passage in the memoir, Conroy writes:

> I would walk far down the beach, often to Bloody Point, where the British once drove a tribe of Indians to the end of the island and slaughtered them, men, women, and children, at the edge of the sea. I used to walk and look at the dead horseshoe crabs, strange prehistoric creatures who simply could not cope with the pollution of the Savannah River and had washed ashore at Yamacraw by the hundreds. The whole beach stunk of death and decaying marine life. At the end of the island I could see the factories belching and puking into the sky. The same factories that had killed the Yamacraw oysters and the economy of the island had not spared the defenseless, clumsy, and harmless horseshoe crabs. (68)

In this moment of reverie, Yamacraw's beach comes to represent the worst of human nature; the island's isolation fails to protect it from genocide and environmental plundering or to insulate it from violence's attendant despair. This moment in Conroy's narrative quickly passes, but its impact lingers in the book. As Conroy pushes for change on the island, there is a sense of the inevitability of history that, like the corrupted oysters and dead horseshoes, rings the island's borders.

This history presents itself in its most complex and most confounding form in the figure of Mrs. Brown, whose pseudonymous recasting in the book functions as a reminder to readers of her racial identity, a source of great—if largely unacknowledged—anxiety for her. Moreover her lack of a first name in the text is indicative of the ways that she guards her personal identity to the point of erasure; throughout the memoir she remains known only in her professional capacity to the Yamacrawans and to Conroy, her lone colleague on the island, and indeed she rarely is seen off school grounds. There is much humor to be mined in Mrs. Brown's rigid adherence to meaningless professional hierarchies, as in the perfect bit of post–*Catch-22* absurdism in which she pulls rank on Conroy, announcing shrilly, "I am the principal," certainly not a terribly meaningful title in a faculty of two (163).

There is also a real pathos associated with Mrs. Brown, however, perhaps exemplified most succinctly in her initial confusion over the role of the principal: when Conroy first arrives on the island, she insists that he is the principal, despite his protests. He explains that "it suddenly struck me that she took it for granted I was principal simply because I was white" (31). Mrs. Brown's understanding of the world is informed by a set of clear, unchallengeable hierarchies that privilege white, male authority; as a black woman, she seems resigned to her diminished potential, and as a teacher she is committed to passing on this legacy of shame. Her speech to the children on the first day of class is indicative of her approach. She tells the gathered students, "Most of you are slow. All of us know that. . . . Your brains are just slow. But you can learn if you work. You are just lazy, lazy, and lazy people just can't get ahead in life. Of course some of you are even retarded, and that is even worse than being lazy. . . . That just means you have to work even harder than the lazy ones. . . . But retarded people need to be pushed and whipped harder than anyone" (26). We recognize that Mrs. Brown's regular humiliation of the kids, which often veers into unthinkable cruelty, and her reliance on regular corporal punishment to reinforce her authority speak to a tragic internalization of the messages of a deeply racist society; despite whatever empathy we may have for her, though, it is also impossible not to see Mrs. Brown's perpetuation of these attitudes as close to criminal.

For Conroy, Mrs. Brown at first represents an unsolvable problem. As he writes, "White guilt, that nasty little creature who rested on my left shoulder, prevented me from challenging Mrs. Brown [on any point]. . . . At this time of my life a black man could probably have handed me a bucket of cow piss, commanded me to drink it in order that I might rid my soul of the stench of racism, and I would have only asked for a straw" (111). He recognizes, too, that his need for redemption does not address the problem of racism but merely his own racial guilt: "It dawned on me that I came to Yamacraw for a fallacious reason," he concedes. "I needed to be cleansed, born again, resurrected by good works and suffering, purified of the dark cankers that grew like toadstools in my past" (111).[8] Conroy is almost wholly paralyzed in his initial dealings with Mrs. Brown: he believes her to be a bad teacher, an ineffectual administrator, and an inflexible colleague, yet he is silenced by his shame as a white man who has both participated in, and benefited from, a racist culture.[9]

Ultimately, though, Conroy realizes that identity and identity politics do not always neatly align, and in fact Mrs. Brown functions as "the unflinching, strong-armed proponent of white values, mores, and attitudes" (155). As his frustration with Mrs. Brown grows, he begins to respond to what might be termed as her unlikely "whiteness," as evinced in his angry response to her repeated demands that he use a strap on his students: "I had a history of not responding well to lousy or pernicious administration, and though I tried to tell myself that she was the boss and I would have to obey her instructions, I would be goddamned if she was going to turn me into an overseer instead of a teacher" (160–61). The identification of Mrs. Brown as an administrator —linking her to the largely white, male school board—and the suggestion that her reliance on corporal punishment aligns her with a plantation overseer represent a complete inversion in Conroy's understanding of race. In finally allowing himself to become angry with Mrs. Brown, he begins to think of the complexities of race in more expansive ways. (Interestingly he later notes that, conversely, it must also have been a "liberating and purifying experience for [Mrs. Brown] to be able to hate a white man" [291].)

Ultimately, however, the conflict between Conroy and Mrs. Brown is never resolved; instead, shortly after the school year comes to a close, Conroy is summarily fired. To some extent his dismissal seems as if it is the inexorable conclusion of his long-simmering struggle with Superintendent Henry Piedmont and Ezra Bennington, yet the firing also feels sudden and deeply offensive. Ostensibly Piedmont had grown tired of paying what he considered to be an exorbitant gas bill to cover Conroy's daily commute to Yamacraw. (To keep expenses down, the school board wanted him to live on the island during the week, which Conroy had done until his wedding to Barbara in October; after that point the long absences from his new family became untenable.) While the economics of Conroy's employment may be a legitimate issue for Piedmont and the board, Conroy suspects that he had long been viewed as "an irritating labor problem" and that the board, grown used to the sort of quiet compliance typified by Mrs. Brown, is uncomfortable with Conroy's demands that they both acknowledge and address the problems that plague the island (259). Moreover, no matter how earnest Conroy's intentions, he readily admits that the "usual bombast and fustian" that mark his communication with administrators tend to put them on the defensive (192).

When he brings his case to the school board after his firing, then, Conroy knows that a deferential approach will be most successful. Indeed, despite his battles with Piedmont over the course of the year, the two have a grudging respect for one another. (Conroy, in fact, neatly echoes his observations about Ezra Bennington when he concedes, "For some reason I realized that I really liked Henry Piedmont" [247].) Yet Conroy ultimately decides not to follow this conservative path, seeing the school board meeting as a chance for advocacy that extends beyond his own case. Speaking to a room packed with family, friends, and a number of his students' parents who have crossed the river to attend, Conroy details the conditions on the island and castigates the school board for their lack of commitment to the children's education. The meeting becomes a raucous spectacle, marked by angry exchanges between Piedmont and Conroy. When Conroy wins, it feels as if it is a moral victory, one that will redefine the community.

But the school board meeting is simply the opening battle in a larger war. Piedmont, humiliated by Conroy's public accusations, waits for an opportunity to fire him on new charges, and when Conroy takes a five-day consulting position with the Desegregation Center of South Carolina as a means of raising money for a student trip to Atlanta, Piedmont accuses him of "disobeying instructions, insubordination, conduct unbecoming a professional educator, and gross neglect of duty" (275–76). He is similarly prepared with heavy artillery when the community once again comes to Conroy's defense, this time threatening Yamacraw parents with jail time after they organize a boycott of the school. With a new sense of commitment, Piedmont prevails in his defense of Conroy's firing both in a board of education review and at a courtroom trial, and thus, with a sense of unsettling finality, Conroy's teaching career comes to an end.

Despite his overwhelming sense of personal despair in the months after he is fired, though, Conroy recognizes that the end of his teaching career is also a marker of the new era that the civil rights movement has brought to the South. The concluding chapter of *The Water Is Wide* moves from the more personal focus of the preceding chapters and, instead, celebrates the change that has inspired unmistakable fear in southerners such as Bennington and Piedmont, Ted Stone, and even Mrs. Brown, whom Conroy identifies as "perhaps the most tragic of all the protagonists in the masque of Yamacraw" (291). In capturing the tone of this change, Conroy returns again to the river as a symbol, but it no longer merely represents the fissure that divides Yamacraw from the world, one that can be bridged only by those brave and committed enough to face its dangers. Instead the river becomes a sign of strength and transformation; he explains that "during the entire period of my banishment and trial, I wanted to tell Piedmont and Bennington that what was happening between us was not confined to Beaufort, South Carolina. I wanted to tell them about the river that was rising quickly, flooding the marshes and threatening the dry land. I wanted them to know that their day was ending. . . . The world was very different now" (290–91). In the memoir's conclusion, then, Conroy puts faith in the "new flow and the new era" that are shaping the South, and he concedes that while the type of revolution he had imagined at the outset of his time on Yamacraw is not always successful, he finds hope in the inevitable power of "gradual and slow change, like the erosion of a high bluff during spring tides" (292). Even monoliths, Conroy suggests in this image, are not immune to the forces of cultural change.

It is with this broad understanding of transformation in mind that Conroy finally reflects on his own role in challenging injustice, conceding, "I don't think I changed the quality of [the Yamacraw children's] lives significantly or altered the inexorable fact that they were imprisoned by the very circumstance of their birth" (292). His assessment is suggestive of a line from "The Water Is Wide," the English folk song from which he borrows the memoir's title, in which the singer plaintively cries, "And I know not if I sink or swim." The ambiguity inherent in Conroy's consideration of his legacy seems fitting: at the conclusion of the narrative, Conroy, like the South itself, finds himself in flux.

Of course the change that he chronicles in *The Water Is Wide* is paralleled by his own transformation, that from teacher to writer, and the story of the memoir's creation, publication, and public reception is as arguably as dramatic as Conroy's account of his year on Yamacraw. His firing attracted national attention, including a story in *Newsweek,* and Conroy "realized that I had a story to tell . . . that had never been written by a white boy in my part of the world."[10] He also had time to tell it; unlike his writing of *The Boo,* much of which was squeezed into weekend and evening hours because of his teaching responsibilities, his work on *The Water Is Wide* was a full-time commitment, the silver lining of his enforced unemployment. The project was not without its pressures, though. In addition to financial anxiety caused by the fact that the Conroys would raise their now three daughters solely on Barbara's teaching salary, Conroy was acutely aware of the burdens of memoir writing. In a journal from the period, he writes: "The beginning is the most difficult part. I have a story to tell, but the thought of putting everything on paper, and telling it the way it really happened, frightens me somewhat." His journals reflect that he grappled, too, with finding his voice: "Can I be human enough? Shit no."[11]

Conroy's doubts were mollified, in part, when he enrolled in a creative writing workshop with James Dickey, who had come to the University of South Carolina two years earlier, and this immersion in the world of poetry was buoying: Conroy writes that "I left class armed with weaponry I needed for my own life among words."[12] Conroy's work on the memoir was also shaped by the fact that three of his former students had come to live with him and his family in Beaufort during the period in which he wrote the book; his continued commitment to them, as well as their "fresh eyewitness accounts" of the year on the island, helped to ground him in the project.[13] Thus, despite the bruises that remained after the battles with the Beaufort School Board and the hesitations of a writer first setting out to tell his own story, Conroy threw himself into the work wholeheartedly: "The chapters came fast and I tried to control the immense anger and hurt I felt inside me. But the words began to speak out for me, and I recognized my own voice and realized I was discovering the voice I would be using for the next fifty years."[14]

The next phase in the manuscript's development seems the stuff of fiction itself. After he had completed a draft of *The Water Is Wide,* Conroy was put in touch with the literary agent Julian Bach, who asked that the manuscript be mailed to him the next day. Conroy, who does not type, was stymied, but Barbara and his mother sprang into action, farming out a single chapter to each of a group of friends and then collecting the typed pages to mail the next day. When Conroy began to assemble the pages as they were returned to him, he realized with some chagrin that "some of those glorious typists who banged out pages for Julian Bach had used onionskin paper, others long yellow sheets, and still others short blue sheets. Since I didn't type, I didn't know about the existence of pica or elite or that kind of typescript that looks like handwriting. Harriet Keyserling had typed her chapter on her personal stationery. The first chapter's pages were numbered one to twenty, the second chapter's one to seventeen, the third chapter's one to twenty-five, and so on."[15]

Despite such an inauspicious start, Bach agreed to represent Conroy, and the manuscript was accepted by Houghton Mifflin. The book's success surprised both Conroy and his publishers: predictably it found loyal fans in teachers across the country—indeed the book functions as a love letter to teachers working in difficult conditions—but *The Water Is Wide*'s wise humor and earnest reflection also struck a chord in a country grappling with issues of race.[16] The book was excerpted in *Time,* and in what would have been an unimaginably heady experience for a new writer, it was then optioned by 20th Century-Fox and made into the film *Conrack,* starring Jon Voight and directed by Martin Ritt, who had previously directed films adapted from works by William Faulkner and Tennessee Williams. It would seem, then, that Conroy's difficult experiences on Daufuskie and his exhausting battles with the school board had resulted in the sort of seamless happy ending only Hollywood could imagine: fired quite publicly only years before, Conroy was now the author of a successful book with a celebrated film adaptation.

In fact, though, the publication of *The Water Is Wide* marked the beginning of a pattern that has repeated itself in some form throughout Conroy's life. In writing about home—in this case about the communities of Daufuskie and Beaufort, and in many of his later books, about family—Conroy disrupted that home so forcefully that it became unrecognizable, and the fallout threw him into despair. In this case he reports that *The Water Is Wide* "caused a firestorm in South Carolina," and Beaufort, once an idyllic refuge, began to feel unwelcoming on good days, overtly hostile on others. "Beaufort had hurt me deeply, and no longer seemed like the place I could spend the rest of my life," he has explained, and he, Barbara, and their daughters moved to Atlanta in 1973.[17]

Reviews of the book were largely positive: writing in the New York Times, Anatole Broyard concluded that "Pat Conroy has a nice, wry perspective and a wholehearted commitment to his job. It's a hell of a job and The Water Is Wide is a hell of a good story." A number of reviews focused not on the book itself but on the larger issues of American education and racial politics. For instance Jim Haskins, known for his own book on teaching in underfunded Harlem schools, published a fairly cutting review in the New York Times, taking particular issue with Conroy's teaching style: "We never really know if Conroy attempted to teach [the students] to read as opposed to remembering information by rote, or if he tried to apply his call-answer technique to the teaching of information more fundamental to their Sea Islands existence."[18]

Conrack, as one might expect, was a more sentimental depiction of Conroy's teaching experiences, and while he had not served as a screenwriter, reviewers' discussions of the film often blurred the line between his memoir and Ritt's film. (Significantly many readers were introduced to Conroy's book after they had seen the film, which complicated their reaction to the two works.) Many of the reviewers, including influential New Yorker critic Pauline Kael, were positive in their assessment, but serious criticisms were also levied against the film in the national press.[19] For example Eugenia Collier wrote in the New York Times that the film "is not really about the Sea Islanders—it is about the young white liberal. . . . Once again, blacks are depicted as the Culturally Deprived, the helpless and the hopeless, awaiting the beneficence of the enlightened and liberal white to lift them from their state of abysmal ignorance."[20] In an interview in the New Orleans Review that focused specifically on Conrack, Conroy addressed criticisms such as Collier's, saying, "There are a lot of white teachers teaching black kids and a lot of black teachers teaching white kids, and if you have to be a certain color in order to get things across, then we are in worse shape than I thought. I spent my whole life fighting that conception, and I just don't want to go back to it now."[21]

In the same interview, Conroy deflects some of the criticism levied against the film by confessing that "Conrack is certainly not a 'now' movie. . . . The film is not a Superfly."[22] Yet The Water Is Wide has persisted well beyond the cultural moment it describes: it was reissued in paperback as recently as 2009; was adapted as a musical and successfully staged at New York's AMAS Repertory Theater in 1987; and served as the basis for a second film adaptation, this one for the Hallmark Channel, in 2006. Even as it speaks to the realities of the South at the close of the 1960s, then, The Water Is Wide remains meaningful in its thoughtful reflection upon the broader ways that power is created and maintained. And while Daufuskie may no longer exist as Conroy depicted it—the island was developed into a series of resort communities in the 1990s—the sort of paradoxes and contradictions that defined his time there continue to exist within the South and, indeed, remain central to Conroy's work in the wake of *The Water Is Wide*.

CHAPTER 3

The Great Santini

After the publication of *The Water Is Wide,* Conroy was ready to approach "the book I was born to write": *The Great Santini* (1976), a fictionalized account of his family's experiences growing up with his abusive marine fighter pilot father.[1] The book is often heralded by critics for its sensitive treatment of a coming-of-age narrative, but in its account of Ben Meecham's attempts to escape the long shadow of his father, the "Great Santini" of the title, and thus come into a form of manhood of his own making, the novel also addresses a number of other themes that emerge as central to Conroy's oeuvre. Most notably *The Great Santini* engages in a complicated consideration of a broader form of paternalistic power, tracing in particular the ways that institutionalized constructions of masculinity shape identity, often warping it to the point of alienation. Moreover, despite the works' very different subjects, *The Great Santini* expands upon *The Water Is Wide*'s exploration of the consolations and corruptions of southern identity and considers the ways in which violence often bridges the gap that exists between them.

The novel opens in a Barcelona hotel toward the close of a raucous farewell party being held for Lt. Col. Bull Meecham after a year-long tour on an aircraft carrier. The party has spiraled out of control, and when a navy captain who is dining at the hotel chastises the marines for being disruptive, Bull leads a plot in which he feigns illness in the middle of the dining room, using mushroom soup to approximate vomit, and then two marines pretend to lap up the "vomit" with spoons in a perverse race. Not surprisingly many of the diners in the restaurant, including the naval officers' wives, become sick themselves. The incident, beginning with the wild party and ending with the grotesque response to the naval officer's assertion of authority, is emblematic of the hypermasculine ethos at the center of the Marine Corps. In wartime the battles in which marines are engaged are clear; out of the field, however, they must invent ways of testing their skill and bravado, often devising contests that cross into the world of the absurd, offensive, and dangerous. To be a marine, we see in *The Great Santini*'s initial scene, is to participate in a culture that does not tolerate weakness of any sort and to exist in a mode of perpetual swagger.

The novel's opening is equally significant in that it demonstrates that the marines' construction of manhood is so exaggerated that, in its distorted form, it more accurately reflects adolescent behavior: Bull's performance with the mushroom soup may be a particularly dramatic example, but it is in keeping with the scatological and phallic jokes, drinking contests, and elaborate pranks that Bull sees as central to the "Old Corps." This blurring of lines between boy-hood and manhood, evinced and underscored in the novel's first pages, exists in parallel to the novel's central narrative, in which Ben must navigate the shifting ground between childhood and adulthood as he approaches graduation from high school. This period is notoriously difficult for any teenager to navigate, of course, but Ben's path toward manhood is especially perilous in that it is relentlessly patrolled by Bull, who seeks to assure himself of his son's basic "toughness" and who simultaneously, if less consciously, also fears his eldest son's growing strength as a sign of his own diminishment. For Ben this classic Oedipal dilemma plays out with a fresh sense of urgency; as graduation nears along with its inevitable conferral of adulthood, Ben must not only come to terms with the complicated dynamic of his own home, but must also decide if he will replicate—and thus tacitly accept—a model of manhood that he claims to abhor by joining the Marine Corps, as his parents expect him to do.[2]

If the novel's opening scene is dedicated to highlighting the powerful constructions of masculinity that will inform the narrative, the chapters that immediately follow introduce an equally important—and similarly fraught—theme in *The Great Santini,* that of home. The family is first introduced to the reader as they wait for Bull's plane to appear after his yearlong Mediterranean tour, a "homecoming" that is inherently ironic because all of the Meechams understand that Bull's arrival, by definition, will fully disrupt that home: in an instructive aside, the third-person omniscient narrator explains that when a father is stationed abroad, the rest of the family experiences "a looseness, a freedom from tension, a time when martial law was suspended. Though a manless house was an uncompleted home, and though the father was keenly missed, there was a laxity and fragile vigor that could not survive his home-coming" (17). Bull's arrival, then, represents a largely unwelcome return to a stricter, more disciplined mode of living. Additionally the Meechams' sense of home will be disturbed by Bull's return in a more literal fashion: now that he has returned from Europe, the family can expect to move to a new post. Indeed as a marine family, the Meechams have no fixed home; instead they are "middle class migrants," moving from base to base as the Corps dictates (25).

Bull alone seems absolutely comfortable with the geographical rootlessness demanded of marines, taking real pleasure in their moves. Within a month of his return, he moves the family from Atlanta, where they have been staying with Lillian's mother, to their next post in Ravenel, South Carolina. Even though Lillian cautions the children that Bull is "easily upset on trips" (26), Bull seems to relish the move: unlike his groggy family, as he wakes up for the trip, his "body [is] alive, vibrant, [and] singing like an electric wire" (22), and once they set off he seems uncharacteristically relaxed for most of the journey. Indeed Bull seems to enjoy the family routines and rituals associated with the move, many of which, like the 2 A.M. start time, the collective singing of the "Marines' Hymn," and the playful exchange of barbs among the family members, are also reflective of the culture of the Marine Corps (26). The trip seems to affirm Bull's identity in many ways: as the sole driver, he is literally and metaphorically "taking the wheel" after his prolonged absence, and he complicates this domestic role by engaging in the "hobby" of running over turtles as he drives, an act of casual violence that functions as an absurdist affirmation of his power (39).

If Bull finds his own identity reified by their regular moves, however, the Meecham children feel the effects of dislocation deeply. Ben, in particular, dreams of "a sense of place, of belonging, and of permanence," and because he was born in Georgia and returned to it whenever he visited his grandmother, "it was the one place he could hold to, fix upon, identify as belonging to him. . . . He lived there only when his father went overseas, but that made no difference to him" (44). This last line, of course, is particularly revealing. The suggestion here is that his father's relative absence should interfere with Ben's acceptance of Georgia as home, but in fact it might be argued that it is living without Bull that allows Ben to feel the expansiveness of being "at home." Not only does his time in Atlanta represent a break from "the washed-out, bloodless Marine bases where he had lived for most of his seventeen years" (44), but it also represents a suspension from the expectations and assumptions of Marine Corps life.

While Ben never explicitly identifies Atlanta—and the notion of home that it embodies—as gendered, Bull sees the entire South as inherently feminized, and more specifically as an extension of Lillian, who, in her studied graciousness and mannered reverence of all things beautiful, is fully entrenched in the myth of the southern belle. Their complex relationship, then, is overlaid onto Bull's understanding of home, and his constant attacks on the South stem in part from his continuing need to exert his authority in their marriage. Bull is quick to denigrate the South whenever he can—in his lexicon Georgia is "the armpit of Dixie" and South Carolina is the "sphincter of America"—and he casually attacks Lillian's shibboleths on a regular basis; he dismisses "Dixie" as "a loser's song," for example (32); calls *Gone with the Wind*, Lillian's favorite film, a "real horsecrap movie" (55); and even shows regular contempt for Okra, the family dog, whose name alone seems to condemn him to a lifetime of Bull's derision. While this sort of South-baiting is almost expected of the Chicago-born Bull, especially given the elevation of trash talk to an art form in the culture of the Old Corps, it is also representative of a deeper sense of mistrust of the "strange separateness" he associates with the region and, by extension, Lillian (45). The battle between North and South plays out in an eternal loop in the Meecham household, often in quiet but potent ways. For example each morning that Bull eats at home, Lillian serves him grits, perhaps the most emblematic of southern foods, and "as was customary in their nineteen years of marriage, he left the grits on his plate untouched, an unexpressed but articulate declaration, rooted in geography, that the society he married into had not assimilated him. . . . What had begun as a joke between them had become a resolute ceremony fraught with competition and even with something deeper, something almost mythological that separated them" (91).

The conflict manifested in this uncomfortable breakfast tableau becomes exaggerated when the family moves to South Carolina and, in the absence of available officer housing, Bull rents a beautiful house in the historic section of Ravenel (32). The house is a true gift to Lillian, and she is moved by Bull's pride in providing her with what he recognizes is the "southern mansion . . . you always wanted to live in" (58). But while the house is a visible marker of Bull's ability to provide for Lillian, it is also represents a risk to him. Not only has he separated himself from the base, where clearly defined hierarchies underscore his authority, but Bull is also actively moving into a space that represents a fuller articulation of Lillian's power; certainly her strength has always been evident, but until her investiture in the Ravenel mansion, it has not been allowed to manifest itself on its own terms. We are told that Lillian "had been reared to inhabit a house as fine as this and only the accidental liaison with a man in love with the Marine Corps had interfered with this consummation" (62). This observation speaks not only to an upbringing that exists apart from—and, it is implied, *above*—Bull's, but the explicitly sexualized rhetoric here suggests the ways in which the house and the southern myth it exemplifies stand in direct competition with Bull. When Lillian is finally allowed to "consummate" her destiny by occupying the house, then, Bull senses that his own manhood risks being undermined.

As soon as they move into the house, Bull actively, if unconsciously, works to redefine domestic spaces as masculine, engaging in strict inspections of his children's rooms and in raucous family "war games" that had become tradition in their base housing. In these scenarios Bull is subsumed almost wholly by his marine persona, and while he injects a sense of camp into his pronouncements of his power—"It is I, Santini. The Great Santini. Soldier of Fortune. Beast of Ravenel. Minister of Death. And the best damn pilot in the Marine Corps" (88) —he remains an emotionally intimidating and physically threatening figure, casting a shadow that persists even when he is out of the house. Conversely Bull tries to replicate domestic rituals in a patriarchal space, choosing to eat breakfast each weekday at Hobie's Grill, a local diner populated by men who spend much of their morning engaged in cheerful denigration of one another. Bull ostensibly makes Hobie's a part of his routine in the interest of marine-civilian relations, but it is apparent that he receives a sense of deep satisfaction from his acceptance into this "closed and grandly intolerant brotherhood" (169).

Yet despite the bombast he displays at home and the comfortable acceptance he finds at Hobie's, Bull is destabilized by his immersion in a fully southern setting, a fact that is evinced in his encounters with Arrabelle Smalls, the woman Lillian hires as the family's maid upon arriving in Ravenel. Lillian has justified the expense by telling Bull that "[a] squadron commander's wife needs a maid" (101), intimating the ways in which Arrabelle occupies a clear place within the military hierarchy, but in fact Arrabelle represents a network of relationships based on gender, race, and region that exist outside of Bull's experience and that challenge his understanding of himself. Bull first encounters Arrabelle without the benefit of Lillian's introduction, and as soon as he sees her on their steps on her first morning of work, he is stymied:

> If there was a single group in America that Bull had difficulty with over the simplest forms of address, a group as mysterious to him as children, it was southern blacks. He had nothing at all to say to them so he generally retreated into his self-aggrandized mythology.
>
> "Stand by for a fighter pilot," Bull boomed at the woman.
>
> "What you say, Cap'n?" the woman answered, turning around to look at Colonel Meecham.
>
> "I am the Great Santini," Bull said, beating one fist against his chest and smiling without confidence. He knew he was making a complete ass out of himself but had no idea how to organize a retreat at this juncture of the conversation. (102–3)

Bull's uncertainty as he addresses Arrabelle is comic, but it is also profoundly revealing. His inclination to infantilize African Americans—they are as "mysterious to him as children"—speaks to Bull's limited understanding of southern history, and it presages the ways in which his own identity is quickly inverted. Almost immediately after meeting Arrabelle, he is engaged in a hollow performance of masculinity, one that might be meaningful among marines but here evacuates him of all power, including the ability to conceive of a "retreat." Moreover Arrabelle's use of the colloquialism *Cap'n* to address Bull unwittingly robs him of his rank, and his identity is further undermined when she observes, "I never work for no Eye-talian family before," severely cutting his Irish pride (103). As a uniformed officer, Bull is a man who quite literally wears his identity on his sleeve, and he has no idea what to do when he is not immediately recognized.

Perhaps the most dramatic inversion of his identity, though, takes place when Arrabelle, in a demonstration of her strength, urges Bull to punch her and then allow her to hit him in return. Bull, not wanting to hit Arrabelle, punches her weakly only out of a sense of courtesy and, perhaps, bewilderment. Like many of Bull and Arrabelle's exchanges, this contest is mined for comedy in the novel, but the sharp irony of Bull's reluctance to hit a woman is not lost in the absurdity of Arrabelle's challenge. Moreover Bull's identity is further subverted when Arrabelle throws her punch, a blow that literally takes his breath away and leaves him reeling. He has dismissed her claim that she is as strong as a man, but Arrabelle's powerful punch calls into question the absolute nature of Bull's physical strength, a quality central to his manhood and, as the nickname "Bull" intimates, his very identity. After their contest Bull tries to dismiss Arrabelle by offering her a dollar to "buy a couple of watermelons," a gesture that is made in the same jesting tone that has marked their exchange thus far, but one that can also be seen as an ugly move to assert his racial and economic dominance. Yet even here Arrabelle bests Bull: after she takes his money, she explains that she is not "mak[ing] a circuit of this neighborhood getting handouts," as he teasingly suggests, but that Lillian has hired her to work for the family (104). Arrabelle's identity cannot be a surprise to Bull, but in introducing herself in this moment, she confirms that she has a clear and identifiable role in the house, a claim that underscores Bull's own destabilization.

Arrabelle also acts as a mirror for Lillian's relationship to the South: immediately upon meeting her, Lillian urges her to sit down, explaining. "We're going to get to be too good of friends for me to be sitting and you to be standing while we're having coffee each morning" (105). The implication of equality in Lillian's overture may be more symbolic than meaningful—both Lillian and Arrabelle understand that their connection is rooted in their identities as employer and employee and that race is a powerful factor in that relationship—but Lillian's warm greeting of Arrabelle is significant in its sharp contrast to Bull's uncertain posturing; unlike Bull, who is unsettled by Arrabelle, Lillian sees her presence as a confirmation of her own identity. Moreover Lillian views Arrabelle as an important ally in the upkeep of the house, telling her that while they are unable to make structural repairs, together they will "apply makeup in the right places when the old girl starts to show her spots and wrinkles" (106). In her employment of this metaphor, Lillian reveals the ways she sees the house as an embodiment of herself; just days before, she deflects a compliment from a neighbor about her beauty, demurring, "I'm not pretty at all. I just have my mother's strong features and I'm good with makeup" (96). For Lillian the house—and Arrabelle's role within it—is central to her self-fashioning.

As important, Lillian sees the family's time in Ravenel as her last chance to impart Ben with a clearer sense of his southern heritage. When Lillian meets Arrabelle's son, Toomer, she rather suddenly asks him if he will take Ben fishing, explaining, "His daddy's a Yankee and never encouraged him to participate in any outdoor sports like hunting and fishing. The men in my family when I was growing up would rather spend their time in the woods than anywhere else. Ben doesn't know what it means to be a southern man" (110). Lillian's request is loaded in many ways, perhaps most significantly in its implied condemnation of the narrow form of masculinity to which Bull subscribes. Equally important, though, is Lillian's desire that Ben learn "what it means to be a southern man" from Toomer specifically. Toomer is not emblematic of the aristocratic South, but rather he inhabits the "dirty South," a place where men fish for sustenance as much as sport, and in addition to his relative poverty, Toomer's African American identity and his physical disabilities—he has a pronounced stutter and a bad leg—further disenfranchise him within southern hierarchies. Thus in fostering a friendship between Toomer and Ben, Lillian seeks primarily to imbue Ben with "a strong feeling about the land, and about the traditions of [our] homeland" (438), but she also hopes that Ben's relationship with Toomer will continue to encourage a sense gentleness in her son, a quality that she pointedly identifies as the one "I have admired the most in men" (216).[3]

Lillian's desire to ground Ben in the values and culture in which she was raised is paralleled by Bull's determination to indoctrinate his eldest son into a form of manhood that discounts—and even mocks—the kindness that Lillian extolls, and their competing interests are particularly apparent on Ben's eighteenth birthday. Lillian recognizes the day with a letter expressing her pride in him and urging him to "follow [his] noblest instincts" and to "be a force for right and good" (216). Bull similarly recognizes the milestone, and he begins the day with a gesture that is equally sentimental when he presents Ben with his own leather flight jacket. The jacket is a powerful symbol of Bull's own manhood, and because leather flight jackets had been retired by the Marine Corps in favor of a lighter nylon version, the now-obsolete uniform speaks in particular to the mythic identity of the Old Corps. It is not too extreme to argue that the jacket is a truly transformative gift, and Ben identifies the experience of wearing it as quasi-religious: after he puts it on, "he could not have felt more changed if he had put on the silks of Father Pinckney, prayed over a piece of unleavened bread, and felt it quiver with the life and light of God" (202). Much of this feeling of the miraculous can be attributed to the unfathomable feats performed by his father and his colleagues, who can "fly faster than any birds, set an army on fire, or reduce a city of a million people to dust and memory" (202), yet Ben's reference to the act of consecration is equally notable in its emphasis on more a prosaic understanding of communion: to wear his father's jacket is to connect with him in a way that had previously been unimaginable.

With this gift bestowed, Bull takes Ben to witness an early-morning, unsanctioned boot-camp drill session in which the new recruits are alternately insulted and threatened by the instructor, Sergeant Hicks, who had come of age in the Corps with Bull. The session ends when Hicks leads the new marines to believe that he has mortally wounded one of their ranks (a friend of Hicks's who is acting as a plant) and then has two of the recruits throw the man in a dumpster to "die," demanding that they ignore the marine's pleas for mercy. It is a particularly brutal piece of theater, and it serves as a dual initiation rite, one in which the marine recruits are bonded to one another through their collective trauma and complicity in the cover-up of the "murder," and a second in which Ben bonds with his father in their shared—and, to Bull's mind, presumably appreciative—witnessing of Hicks's performance. In inviting him to be in on the "joke," then, Bull is recognizing Ben as a man, a fact that is echoed when Hicks playfully notes that Ben is "old enough to be part of this platoon now" (209). Yet Hicks's rather benign observation and Ben's good-natured dismissal of his tacit invitation also contain the uneasy suggestion that even as Bull congratulates Ben on his new manhood, he also recognizes that his son has not yet been tested in any meaningful way.

In fact this simultaneous celebration of and challenge to Ben's manhood marks almost all of Ben and Bull's exchanges. For instance Bull takes Ben to the Officer's Club on his birthday to buy him "a man's drink," yet Ben becomes so drunk that Bull must carry him home as if he were an infant (220). Indeed even the message inherent in the gift of the flight jacket is marked by paradox: its obsolescence, which imbues the jacket with special value, also ensures that Ben can never earn one of his own. If he is to follow in his father's footsteps and become a fighter pilot, the flight jacket he will receive is a "nylon pretender," a synthetic facsimile that has been entirely "bled of [the] glamour or romance" of the real thing (201). Moreover Bull has cautioned Ben that he can only wear the leather flight jacket "around the house or at night," a reminder that in the eyes of others—and perhaps Bull himself—this inheritance is unearned (199).

To some extent these kinds of inconsistent messages about identity are inherent to the process of becoming an adult; the transition from youth to adulthood is never a linear one. In *The Great Santini,* however, they are often the result of Bull's ambivalence about Ben's impending manhood, which serves as an uncomfortable reminder of the inevitability of own decline. Bull faces any number of challenges associated with aging, including a troubling sense of uncertainty about his own legacy within the Marine Corps. Before the family moves to Ravenel, he has been passed over for promotion to full colonel, and his post in South Carolina represents his last good chance to achieve this rank, a source of deeply felt, if unexpressed, anxiety for Bull. Moreover evidence of Bull's aging body litters the text, from the shortcuts he must take to complete his morning workouts to the "act of semi-strangulation" he engages in to occupy a dress uniform better fitted for his younger self (232). Physical challenges, then, take on an even greater significance to Bull, and when Ben finally beats his father in a game of one-on-one shortly after they have moved to Ravenel, Bull's violent response is not simply a reflection of the fact that he has been physically eclipsed by his son but is grounded a sense that he has suffered an unimaginable loss of power. He responds by contesting the outcome, kicking Lillian, and then telling Ben, "You get smart with me, jocko, and I'll kick you upstairs with your mother so you pussies can bawl together" (131). His own sense of masculinity undermined, Bull seeks to deny Ben's manhood, both by equating him with female genitalia—a quite conscious choice given Bull's expansive catalog of blue language—and by demonstrating that Ben is unable to protect Lillian when Bull chooses to hurt her.

Ben's high school basketball games become a space in which Bull's paradoxical attitudes toward his son are writ large: on one hand Bull dutifully attends every game, offering encouragement and advice beforehand and even inviting other marines to attend. In this regard he seems to take real pride in Ben, viewing his son's success as an extension of his own days on the court. Despite his genuine enthusiasm, though, for the most part Bull is a nuisance at the games, regularly showing up drunk and making catcalls when Ben doesn't play in a way that meets his expectations. In one of the most powerful scenes in the novel, Bull urges Ben on to violence after he has been knocked down by an opposing player, Peanut Abbott, screaming, "You better get that little bastard or you don't come home tonight! I'll beat your ass if you don't get that little bastard! You hear me boy?" (365). Until this exchange Ben has been having one of the best games of his career, and he has been matched with an opposing player, Wyatt Sanders, whose level of play has elevated Ben's game. Ben feels that in their heightened sense of competition, he and Sanders "were honoring each other and celebrating each other's gifts. It was a feeling, a tenderness in the sweetly savage brotherhood of athletics that came very seldom" (364). Ultimately, however, it is Bull's decidedly bitter brand of savagery that wins out, and Ben, "dar[ing] not disobey" the power of his father's rage, breaks Abbott's arm (366).

The consequences are immediate: Ben is bathed in shame, is summarily dismissed from the school's athletic program, and is abandoned by the college scouts who had attended the game. Yet the significance of this scene extends beyond its illustration of the ways in which Bull's model of manhood is an uneasy fit for Ben. In acting on Bull's belief that one must demonstrate physical dominance or yield all power, Ben not only loses his authority on the court but within his relationship with his father as well: he is now barred from the sport in which he is better than his father; he is separated from his coaches, a group of men he has historically viewed as "unruined fathers" and thus looked to as crucial foils to Bull; and he is limited in the colleges he might attend and thus more dependent upon his father's vision of his future (256). While he certainly served as an instigator, Bull did not orchestrate these consequences; instead there is real truth in the assessment made by Ben's principal, the stern but sympathetic Mr. Dacus, that they result from the fact that Ben "doesn't have the guts to tell his father to go take a flying jump when that father is just about as wrong as a father can possibly be" (367).

In a series of scenes that build to the novel's climax, Ben ultimately does defy Bull, and it is in this choice that Lillian's and Bull's constructions of manhood are finally joined for Ben. The first of these scenes takes place after a crescendo of violence in the novel, a pattern that will become a hallmark of Conroy's fiction. Ben's best friend, Sammy Wertzberger, has taken a date to a notorious make-out spot outside of town, a space that is first identified as fraught in its combination of race, sex, and violence when, earlier in the novel, Sammy tries to blackmail a married police officer whom he and Ben find with an African American woman there. Sammy's return visit is marked by an even more catastrophic combustion of these factors: his date is pulled from the car and raped by an unknown black man, and the town of Ravenel is suddenly engaged in a manhunt that ignites racial tensions. Toomer is caught in the frenzied atmosphere after Red Pettus, a member of "the meanest upriver family of all" breaks several of the jars of honey that Toomer sells in a public display of Toomer's powerlessness (161). Toomer, however, responds unexpectedly: he is able to grab Red and trap him in the tire of his wagon, only releasing him after Red screams for help and a crowd that is largely sympathetic to Toomer urges him to let Red go.

Later that night Arrabelle calls Ben, fearing that Red might retaliate after his humiliation and worrying that Toomer is alone, and thus entirely vulnerable, in the abandoned bus in which he lives. Ben calls his father, who is on duty at the air station, and Bull promptly forbids him from going to Toomer's aid. Ben goes anyway, but it is too late: when he arrives Red is dead and Toomer is mortally wounded. Regardless of his intention to save Toomer in an act of sensational heroism, Ben's true act of bravery is much quieter: he has defied his father. It is significant, though, that in doing so Ben also recognizes that he is emulating Bull. When Bull realizes that Ben has gone to Toomer's bus, he abandons his post at the marine base, the first time he has done so in his career. When he finds Ben, he immediately hits him, berating him for "disobeying a direct order" (413). Ben notes, however, that in leaving his post to rescue him, Bull has also broken rank and explains that he went to Toomer's aid in part because "Santini would have done it" (413). On its surface, then, the scene is driven by an almost perfect symmetry, one in which both Bull and Ben defy the rules that dictate masculine hierarchies in order to honor the higher spirit of the code to which they subscribe. Their twin choices also represent a potential shift in their relationship: in leaving the base to save Ben, Bull for the first time defies the observation made by Mr. Dacus that Bull "believes in the institution over the individual even when the individual is his own child" (388). Similarly Ben recognizes one of the essential redeeming qualities in Bull's construction of manhood when he emulates his fierce bravery.

Yet despite the satisfying nature of these parallels, Conroy complicates this scene in a number of ways, unsettling its suggestion of tidy resolution even as he creates it. First, although Ben explains his decision to try to help Toomer by explaining that "Santini would have done it," in fact he has acted in large part because he has been shamed by his sister. When Bull first tells Ben that he cannot go out to Toomer's bus, Mary Anne goads Ben into action, repeating a pattern of behavior witnessed earlier in the novel. Months before Ben and Mary Anne had stumbled across a scene in which Red was demanding that Sammy, who is Jewish, profess his love of Hitler. Ben, who had not yet befriended Sammy, would have preferred to ignore the scene, but he was forced to intercede when Mary Anne offered to take up Sammy's cause herself. In this instance Mary Anne again says she will save Toomer if Ben will not. Ben's response here is an interesting one: just as he had in the confrontation between Red and Sammy, he says that he will engage in the conflict "because if something happened to [Mary Anne] Dad would never quit punching me," but he also displays a rare and venomous anger toward his sister, calling her a "sickening little bitch" and telling her, "I know what you're doing and it really pisses me off" (406). What Mary Anne is doing, although Ben does not acknowledge it, is living up to the ideals of manhood expressed by Bull in her instinctive bravery and also those identified by Lillian in her stated desire that Ben stand up for what is "right and good." In short Mary Anne supplants Ben as the family's "golden boy," as she often identifies him, and thus his anger is reflective of his own shame rather than righteousness, and his decision to help Toomer is spurred as much by Mary Anne's recognition of his impotence as it is rooted in his sense of duty.

The impact of the scene is further complicated by Bull's refusal to directly acknowledge Ben's act of bravery. Upon his arrival he berates Ben for several moments, belittling him by repeatedly calling him "sweet pea" and threatening him with punishment. His barrage is only interrupted when he finally notices Toomer's body. Thus while Ben and Bull operate in parallel with one another, Bull never recognizes their mutual impulses and, by extension, Ben's manhood. The flight jacket Bull has given Ben serves to underscore this lack of connection. When he first receives the jacket, Mary Anne is dismissive of the gift, sourly noting that it "will be good to wrap fish in or cover a body if we ever witness a murder" (216). Her remark proves prescient, as Ben does indeed cover Toomer with it after he has died. On its face this act is a way of decorating Toomer as a fallen soldier, but in the context of Mary Anne's statement, the jacket also speaks to the hollowness of the constructions of masculinity that have led to this moment: Red's misguided sense of honor has brought about his own death and Toomer's, and Bull's interpretation of a masculine code keeps him from connecting with his son. It is telling, then, that as the scene concludes, the jacket is ruined.

It is in yet another moment of violence that Ben is truly able to redefine his relationship with his father. Bull has attended Mess Night, a celebration of marine fraternity that is marked by a series of dramatic contests of linguistic and physical bravado, and when he arrives home is he both terrifically drunk and intoxicated by his own myth. Lillian confronts him, and when Bull savagely attacks her, the children come to her aid and are injured as well. Ben is the last to join the fracas, in part because of an essential and legitimate fear of his father's fists, and in part because of a more subtle, but equally terrifying, emotional component to the situation: both Ben and Bull understand that Ben is "the only child who could influence the battle at all" (426), and accordingly Bull will reserve a special ferociousness for him in this role. This quickly becomes evident when Bull tries to strangle Ben, and surrounded by bloodied and disoriented family members, the fight is reduced to "Ben and his father, eye to eye, as intimate as lovers" (427). Ben is aware of this connection, and even after Bull violently and repeatedly bangs his head against a wall, he is unable to strike out against his father, knowing instinctively that "he could not hit the face of the father that would be the face of his father for all time" (428). Even when he is most consumed with hatred for his father, Ben is aware of something larger that informs their violent dance.

Ben gives name to this in *The Great Santini*'s emotional climax. After the fight Bull stumbles from the house, and not long after Lillian becomes worried that he has passed out somewhere and charges Ben to go and retrieve him. Ben resists, but only weakly: he and his mother have survived this scene many times already, and in this instance they both seem ready to abandon the familiar script in which she earnestly—but ultimately emptily—promises to leave Bull. When Ben finds Bull on the Lawn, a common area near their house, both men have been evacuated of their rage: Ben is physically and emotionally exhausted, and Bull is so drunk that he cannot walk unassisted. Looking at Bull, an entirely pathetic figure at this point, Ben startles himself by professing his love for his father. It is a moment of shocking power: Bull pulls back as if stung, made uncomfortable, perhaps, by the naked emotion of the moment but also deeply shamed by his own failures. As Ben repeats his assertion of love again and again, Bull tries to run from Ben, but, still drunk, he runs "in an agonizingly circuitous pattern, weaving and stumbling, falling once, but immediately on his feet again, running slowly, unable to escape anything" (431). His physical uncertainty here stands in sharp contrast to the image of a man who always moves with purpose—as a basketball player, as a pilot, and as a brawler. In this moment Bull is truly overwhelmed, transformed from Bull Meecham, the Great Santini, to a common ox, a fact that is underscored in the image of Ben running past his father, "slap[ping] him on the rump in passage, and turn[ing] him like a steer" (431). Significantly Bull never tells Ben that he loves him in return, but Ben expresses no need for this affirmation. Instead he is empowered by the freedom he experiences in his own recognition of love and its effect on Bull.

The novel closes with Bull's death, an event that is foreshadowed in the novel's opening pages. The circumstances of Bull's death—and Ben's response to it—are less predictable, however. Bull is on a routine flight when a fire in his engine forces an emergency landing. Rather than crash in a populated area, he chooses to punch out over water, a choice that gives him the slimmest odds for survival. It is a quick death, at least textually: in one moment Bull is engaging in an exchange with the tower that takes place in the spare language of pilots in which "all fat had been trimmed, all excess removed" (451), and in the next Bull is simply silent. His decision, which is rooted in a desire to privilege the lives of "families like my family" (453) above his own, is given no further explication, and this lacunae is in keeping with Bull's rigid persona and simultaneously is profoundly moving in its evocation of other absences in the text, most notably Bull's inability to express love for Ben.

Bull's death also represents the impossibility of Ben's forging a fuller sense of resolution with his father, though, and when he joins the search party after the accident to look for his father, it is clear that while there may be a chance of finding Bull's body, discovering him in a more meaningful way is now futile.[4] It is not surprising, then, that in the wake of Bull's death Ben finds himself tortured by his own ambivalence: "He realized that he lived in a Santiniless world now and he trembled when he thought that he was, in many ways, relieved that his father was dead. It made him angry that a burden was lifted from him at his father's funeral and it made him suffer" (469). Yet Ben's relief, born of a hatred of his father that he has nurtured for most of his life, is only one aspect of his feelings toward Bull, and as the family leaves Ravenel for Atlanta after the funeral, he recognizes that while much of his anger remains, he is also overwhelmed by "the love of Santini" (471). This observation, contained in the novel's lyrical last line, offers a different form of relief for Ben, and he takes pleasure in it in part because he recognizes the love he feels as true and, more subtly, because in allowing himself to love his father, he is able to reject the sort of rigid thinking that kept the relationship from being satisfying while Bull was alive. In the final pages of the novel, the lines between love and hatred, boyhood and manhood, and home and displacement are blurred in ways that allow for the kind of possibility that Ben has always sought.

As is true elsewhere in *The Great Santini*, though, Conroy's characters' epiphanic moments are more complex than they appear. In this instance, even as Ben is imagining a God who can "translate" his accusations of hatred for his father as expressions of love, he also "knew the hatred would return," potentially supplanting that love (471). And while Ben clearly finds comfort in assuming Bull's role as the family leaves Ravenel—he leaves in the middle of the night and wears Bull's "nylon pretender," for instance—in imitating his father, he treads dangerous ground. Earlier in the novel, Mary Anne makes the fairly damning prediction that "you'll go to some two-bit southern college and then go into the Marine Corps after you graduate. . . . Slowly, all that's good about you will dissolve over the years and you'll begin believing all the stuff Dad believes and acting like Dad acts" (196). Ben's response to Mary Anne—"I'm not going to be a Marine! I'm not! I'm not! I'm not!" (197)—is an almost perfect echo of Quentin Compson's famous insistence in *Absalom, Absalom!* that he does not hate the South: "I dont hate it. . . . I dont. I dont!"[5] Both characters' plaintive declarations are revealing of an overwhelming ambivalence, but they also point to the inevitability of their allegiances. For Quentin, the South will always be home. And accordingly Ben's response to Mary Anne suggests that he will always be father-haunted, an assumption that the novel's conclusion only seems to underscore.

Interestingly, in this conversation with Ben, Mary Anne predicts a similarly grim fate for herself, one that reveals a great deal about the position of women in the novel: "I'll be married to some creep, having children and wishing I was dead," she prophesies (196). Mary Anne has described her mother's life here, and even though she resembles Lillian in very few ways, she accurately captures the limitations of womanhood more broadly. Mary Anne has grown up largely neglected by her father, who "doesn't pay attention to anything that doesn't wear a uniform or have a jump shot" (195), and has been told by her mother that "[a] woman has one job. To be adorable. Everything else is just icing" (348). This is an especially cruel assessment for Mary Anne, who is neither conventionally beautiful nor interested in the sort of charm that her mother has perfected and thus is largely silenced both in the larger culture and in her family.

Mary Anne, then, is often reduced to a form of communication that only she and Ben, her chief confidante, can understand. We see this early in the novel when she begins to sob as the family approaches Ravenel for the first time and she thinks about the consequences of yet another move. Bull predictably demands, "You better get her to stop, Lil. I can't stand boo-hooing," and Lillian urges Mary Anne, "If you have a lemon, make lemonade" (50–51). Bull's gruff posturing and Lillian's clichés speak to their shared desire to silence Mary Anne's outburst: Bull cannot tolerate dissention, and Lillian is uncomfortable whenever the facades she has constructed are challenged. Mary Anne, however, finds a language that both incorporates and transcends her parents': she pulls a silver teaspoon pilfered from her mother's silver service from her purse, catches her tears, and flings them at the back of her father's head. The move, while perhaps melodramatic, is a perfect bit of symbolism: by "bombing [Bull] with tears" (51), Mary Anne becomes a soldier in a war of emotion, and by employing her mother's silver as her weapon, she reclaims the conventional symbol of ladyhood as her own.[6]

Throughout the novel Mary Anne is constantly searching for a language in which she can be heard, often turning to obscure or profane approaches: she employs a secondhand copy of James Orchard Halliwell's *Dictionary of Archaic and Provincial Words* to find descriptors of her family's behavior, for instance, knowing that when confronted with an unknown word—and a possible insult—they will ask her to define it, thus granting her a chance to explain her selection. And in a particularly poignant scene, she engages in a bizarre and humiliating performance when Bull ignores her plea to "have a conversation. . . . Just you and me," dismissing her by stating, "You're a simple form of Meecham. You're a girl. Now scram" (350–51). She dances around him suggestively and then tells him she is pregnant by "[a] huge, fat-lipped, kinky-haired Negro named Rufus" and adds that he is a "pacifist homosexual," a "dwarf," "crippled," and "retarded" (352). Here Mary Anne reveals her desperation to engage Bull in any way; because he refuses to talk with her, she tries to inspire his focused anger instead, attention he continues to deny her.[7]

Ultimately, then, Mary Anne is a largely silenced figure, one doomed to speak in dead languages or to shout into a vacuum. Lillian, too, suffers—we are given regular glimpses of the ways in which she has been wounded throughout the novel—but unlike her daughter she is also able to find security in the orthodoxies of polite silences; her early training as a southern belle has prepared her well for life as a marine wife, a culture that demands that women will be viewed as "appendages, roses climbing on the trellises" (240), and, as crucially, to find power within this role. Mary Anne, conversely, insists upon a fierce, if irreverent, form of autonomy, and as a result she finds herself alienated in a culture that has no meaningful way of accommodating her voice. Thus while *The Great Santini* is preoccupied with the crippling burden created by the rigidities of masculinity, it also acknowledges the ways in which women are immured in a set of inviolable myths.

This observation becomes more nuanced in Ben's recognition at the close of the novel that he is complicit in Mary Anne's anguish. Throughout the novel their shared sensibility has seemingly saved them from overwhelming isolation, and Ben even takes Mary Anne to their prom in what is both a gesture of real affection and a demonstration of the ways their relationship transcends social expectations. Yet as he takes the wheel of the family car after Santini's death, Ben fleetingly realizes that his own desire to have it both ways—to be the eager beneficiary of his sister's cynical wisdom while maintaining his status as the genially obedient "golden boy"—has ensured that Mary Anne is without a genuine ally: "He had always thought that Mary Anne had been harmed by the coldness of her father and the beauty of her mother. It was only lately that he was having small moments of clarity, of illumination, and seeing himself for the first time as the closest of Mary Anne's enemies, the kindest of her assassins" (469). Ben is quickly distracted by other thoughts, but this recognition of his own participation in Mary Anne's marginalization is a powerful moment in the text, and in subsequent books Conroy repeatedly examines the unintended consequences of white male privilege.

The Great Santini was a remarkable success—the novel was immediately praised for both its unflinching depiction of military life and its fast-paced storytelling in papers such as the *San Francisco Examiner* and the *Boston Globe*—yet its writing and publication had devastating consequences for Conroy. He has explained that writing the novel caused him to confront his childhood in ways that he had previously avoided, and "instead of granting me a portion of strength and satisfaction, the novel felt like a blood-letting, an auto-da-fé, or a crown of thorns."[8] After completing the manuscript, he spent six months in the grips of an unrelenting depression, making a serious suicide attempt in 1975.[9] But Conroy's personal anguish was just the beginning of the pain the novel would cause. *The Great Santini* also demanded that his family confront their shared past, and Conroy's unwillingness—or perhaps inability—to warn them of the novel's content prior to its publication magnified their shock and anger. While his brothers rallied to his aid—he writes that "I could not ask for more valiant safekeepers of my point of view"—Conroy's mother, Peggy, was fierce in her condemnation of the book, identifying it as a betrayal of the family, and her complaints were echoed in a series of searing accusations phoned in by Conroy's relatives.[10]

Don Conroy's response to the novel was the most dramatic of all of Conroy's family members, but it took an unexpected form. After seeing himself reflected in Bull Meecham, he disappeared for several days, prompting Conroy's relatives to charge that Pat had driven his father to suicide, an accusation he feared might be true. When Don reappeared, however, he did so with a letter in hand, and while he told Pat that the book was "a worthless piece of shit," the letter was act of unexpected conciliation.[11] The letter was addressed to all seven of his children and was sent to his Chicago relatives as well, and in it Don explained that he "was deeply touched" by *The Great Santini*, writing that "I was totally absorbed and encountered every emotion as, reading very slowly,"—a joke at his own expense—"life with father unfolded in this work of fiction. It was as though I knew some of the characters personally. . . . I thought the book was great. . . . But how do you go about the task of telling your son and his family that you are profoundly grateful and extremely proud of his latest literary endeavor."[12] While Don Conroy would never acknowledge his abuse of his family, often cheerfully dismissing Conroy's depiction of his brutality as the work of an "overactive imagination" over the years, his gesture in the wake of the novel's publication was enormously meaningful to Conroy and allowed the men to approach their relationship with a new spirit of (wary) generosity.[13]

As *The Water Is Wide* had been, *The Great Santini* was quickly optioned by Hollywood, and the film, directed by Lewis John Carlino and starring Robert Duvall as Bull Meecham, functioned not only as confirmation of the deep appeal of Conroy's narrative but also acted as a vital balm after the damaging writing process. The movie was filmed in Beaufort, and in a surreal blending of lived experience, fiction, and filmmaking, many of the scenes were shot in the spots where the events that inspired them had actually occurred, allowing Conroy and his family to become witnesses to their own histories in a way that they might never have predicted. Moreover by the time *The Great Santini* began filming, the domestic turmoil that had followed the book's publication

had quieted a bit: Don Conroy had embraced the unlikely celebrity that accompanied his identity as Santini, regularly signing books with Pat, and after
her divorce from Don, which she had initiated shortly after his retirement in
1973, Peggy had remarried. While she still felt enormously resentful of Don,
she was also finding that she could create a different kind of life with her new
husband, John Egan. Thus while the filming and the movie's release were not
without painful moments—*Santini* triggered the sorts of waves of jealousy and
resentment in Beaufort that *The Water Is Wide* had—its release coincided with,
and contributed to, a period of relative peace within the Conroy family. Conroy
writes that "the harrowing story of the Conroy family found a form of mysterious healing when the movie *The Great Santini* was loosed to the world."[14]

CHAPTER 4

The Lords of Discipline

For his second novel, *The Lords of Discipline* (1980), Conroy returned to his experiences at the Citadel, the southern military academy that had also been the subject of *The Boo,* a book he has identified as *"The Lords of Discipline in embryo."*[1] Certainly Conroy's depiction of Citadel life, and in particular his sketch of the assistant commandant of cadets, Lt. Col. Nugent Courvoisie— "the Boo"—are echoed and expanded in *The Lords of Discipline,* in which they are thinly disguised as Carolina Military Institute and Col. Thomas Berrineau—"the Bear"—respectively. In the decade between the books' publications, though, Conroy had honed his voice as a writer: while *The Boo* has the feeling of an assemblage of stories that have been "dashed off quickly," as he has acknowledged, *The Lords of Discipline* represents his confidence as a writer. Conroy has explained that it was during the writing of this novel that "I realized that I could finally make a sentence sound exactly how I wanted it to sound."[2]

The plot of *The Lords of Discipline* is ostensibly centered on protagonist Will McLean's charge to aid the first black cadet at Carolina Military Institute, Tom Pearce, in finishing his first year at the college.[3] Colonel Berrineau has assigned Will, a senior, to act as a liaison between Pearce and himself, giving Pearce a means to reach out when "things get out of control" (39). The plebe year is a notoriously brutal experience for all cadets: the upper-class cadre takes it upon itself to run out any "knob" it identifies as weak, employing a brutal hazing system that relies on a combination of seemingly endless formations, sweat parties, and verbal and physical abuse.[4] Even the steeliest of plebes find that they can be broken when the cadre's wrath is turned on them—in an extended flashback, Will equates the hazing that is doled out to "psychic rape"— and given the pervasive racism on campus, the Bear has predicted that the cadre will go to extraordinary lengths to force Pearce to resign (168). Moreover he is concerned about the possible existence of a secret society on campus called the Ten, which, according to a campus historian, is defined largely by its oath "to make sure that no one graduates who is unworthy to wear the ring" (315). The group exists as a spectral entity on campus, intimidating in both its mission and its supposed connection to powerful alumni. If the cadre itself suggests the vulnerability of those who cannot succeed according to its image of itself, the Ten takes such a power to a terrifying extreme.

While this plotline, first introduced in the novel's opening pages, dominates the second half of the book, taking numerous twists as Will both uncovers and confronts the Ten, in fact much of *The Lords of Discipline* is equally concerned with Will's ambivalent relationship to "the Institute," as the college is called by the cadets. By almost all definitions, he is an unconventional cadet: he is an English major at a school that views the liberal arts with a deep suspicion; he is vocal in his skepticism of many of the most scared traditions of the Institute, including the violent hazing of freshmen that is encouraged by its current president, General Durrell; and he is a reluctant soldier, eschewing the behaviors that would allow for military promotion—he is still a private in his senior year—and choosing not to enlist in the Vietnam War. Yet even though he relishes his identity as the school's resident "Bolshevik" and regularly asserts that he has no desire to be tested and tortured in the interest of becoming a "Whole Man," the Institute's term for its graduates, Will is indeed searching for the kind of validation the Institute can provide, a sort of paternal sanction of manhood.

Will notes that he has attended the college because of a promise he made to his dying father, and he is not alone in his desire to live up to his father's ideal of masculinity: throughout the novel he encounters any number of cadets who have enrolled in the Institute as a way of pleasing their own fathers. Tradd St. Croix, one of Will's roommates, for example, candidly tells Will that "I want to make my father glad that I'm his son for the first time in his and my lives (31)." Similarly John Poteete, a plebe who is ultimately driven to suicide during Will's senior year, explains that his father, an Institute graduate, "was happier here than he ever has been since" (111) and contends that even though he himself is miserable at the school, "I could never go home to Dad as a quitter" (112). The Institute, then, functions as a surrogate father to its cadets in a period of crucial transition, and in endorsing their manhood, it provides them with a new way of defining their relationships to their biological fathers. Even as Will marvels at the absurdity of such a system—he thinks of the causalities of war and "wonder[s] how many humans have died because sons wanted to prove themselves worthy of their fathers" (89)—he also recognizes its powerful allure, and to some extent his resolution to graduate is emblematic of the same sort of desperate need for paternal acceptance that he identifies in Tradd and Poteete.

This desire for approbation extends beyond its most obvious Freudian readings, though, and speaks to larger cultural expectations. In a study of southern masculinity, scholar Trent Watts has pointed out that white southern men are taught that "manhood must be learned through rites of initiation and passage, and must be lived and displayed to one's peers and others in order to be fully realized."[5] To become a man, in other words, a southerner must not only meet the challenges associated with the archetypal quest toward adulthood but also must undergo these tests publicly and must accept a communal assessment of his worthiness. Given this understanding, the Institute, which is dependent upon a relentless system of self-policing within the corps, provides an almost perfect testing ground for southern manhood. Indeed while cadets at the Institute are operating under a set of rules common to all military experience, they also recognize that they are participating in a system that is designed not merely to "make men" but to "[make] Southerners" and, even more explicitly, "Southern gentlemen," as Will observes (176). The Institute's model of the Whole Man, defined by moral, physical, and intellectual accomplishment, is patterned on the ideal of the gentleman as much as it is on the hero, and thus is as deeply informed by the ideals of southern manhood—and its implicit gendered, racial, and class hierarchies—as it is by military values.

This overlap between southern and military masculinities is most clearly exemplified in the notion of honor, one of the central themes of *The Lords of Discipline*. The Institute's honor code and the consequences for its violation are clear and succinct: any student found guilty of "lying, stealing, cheating, or of tolerating those who did" (12) is not only expelled but also drummed out in a brutal ceremony that concludes with his complete erasure from Institute history; the name of a cadet who has been banished can never be spoken aloud by another cadet. Will, whose career at the Institute has been otherwise undistinguished, has been elected to the Honor Court, a role that he embraces with great earnestness. While he is mistrustful of many of the rituals that have been designed to enforce a code of ethics, including the "Walk of Shame" required of students who have been expelled for honor violations, Will has deep faith in the honor code itself, noting wryly that he is "chock-full" of the mandated "integrity, sobriety, and honesty" required for its enforcement (12).

Given the Institute's rigid ethical standards and Will's own investment in the notion of honor, it is fairly surprising that the ideal remains hazy to him. When he is asked to define the term by General Durrell, who is looking merely for an appropriately enthusiastic reply, Will confesses, "I'm not certain what honor is. I've been thinking about it all summer, but I'm not absolutely sure what it is or who of my friends has or does not have it" (53). Similarly when he addresses the plebe class to lecture them on the value of the honor code, he finds that his didacticism takes on unexpected qualities of farce: "Over and over again I repeated the word 'honor,' until it became like a pulse beat of my speech. The abstraction defeated me, strangled me in its maddening inexpressibility. . . . I sounded like a minor character in a flawed and cheaply produced operetta who delivers charmingly absurd recitations that have no meaning" (84).

Will's uncertainty here functions to highlight ironies in the plot's development: for instance General Durrell, who chastises Will for failing to define honor, is later revealed to be a wholly ignoble figure, and Will's claim that he does not know "who of my friends has [honor] or does not have it" foreshadows the ways his roommates will confound his expectations. But Will's confusion also speaks to the inherent complexity of southern honor, which both intersects with and eclipses military constructions of honor. Cultural historian Bertram Wyatt-Brown has observed that honor "provide[s] a means to restrict human choices, to point to a way out of chaos." Consequently in the antebellum period southern honor became crucial to defending the status quo, often deviating from conventional notions of communal ethics so that it could more easily "[coexist] with violence and the complacent subjection of so-called inferiors."[6] Wyatt-Brown is referring to the practice of slavery here, of course, but the brutality and casual oppression he cites as warping constructions of antebellum honor are also apt in describing many of the questionable behaviors that the Institute has identified as defensible. Moreover his identification of honor as equally invested in perpetuating specific codes of social conduct and in shaping individual morality succinctly captures the paradoxes that Will, in his naiveté, struggles to understand. His earnest acceptance of honor as a simple ideal is repeatedly challenged throughout the novel, and ultimately his manhood is defined not by his successful completion of the Institute's grueling trials but by his ability to identify which components of the Institute's form of honor are indeed "absurd recitations that have no meaning" and which are truly meaningful.

Interestingly Will first comes to understand the consequences of southern honor outside of the Institute's walls in the city of Charleston, where his experiences function as a crucial parallel narrative to his experiences as a cadet. Of his three roommates, Will is closest to Tradd St. Croix, the scion of one of Charleston's leading families. In Tradd he finds a thoughtful and clever companion and, by chance, a surrogate family: Will is welcomed into the St. Croix home and happily spends time with Tradd's parents, Abigail and Commerce, even when Tradd is elsewhere. Commerce, who is unsettled by Tradd's relative effeteness, is delighted to talk to Will about sports, and Abigail takes pleasure in teaching Will about the history of Charleston. As Will notes, "A passing knowledge of

the Tradd-St. Croix mansion was a liberal education in itself," and he is happy
to serve as Abigail's willing student, soaking up both her lessons and her attention (27). Despite the ease of their relationship, though, Will understands that
the welcome the St. Croixs extend to him cannot erase his stigma as an outsider:
Charleston holds anyone not born into its history at long embrace, and while
the St. Croixs seem unconcerned by Will's Irish Catholic background, his origins, compounded by his affiliation with the Institute, condemn him to a status
as an outsider.

Despite the ways that the city is closed to him, however, many aspects of
Charleston bear an unlikely similarity to the Institute. Will's claim that Charleston is a place that is "distorted by its own self-worship" (3) is one that could certainly be made of the Institute, for instance, and even the city's storied gardens
and historic houses, whose beauty seems to stand in stark contrast to the Institute campus's bland utilitarianism, are marked by an unforgiving sense of order
reminiscent of the Institute's ethos: Will notes, for example, that rather than
displaying a lush riot of native plants, a typical Charleston garden "[extolls] the
virtues of discipline in its severe sculptured rows and regulated islands of green
and bloom" (23). Moreover Will finds that the most revered of the city's historic
mansions are "chilly and remote in an ambiance of . . . conscious perfection"
(288). As impressive as the houses may be, their adherence to an aristocratic
Charlestonian aesthetic denies them any sense of individuality in much the same
way that the Institute's dress grays and buzz cuts make one cadet superficially
indistinguishable from another. Thus even as he is conscious of being excluded
from Charleston society, Will is intimately familiar with the "tyrannical need for
order and symmetry" (3) that he senses beneath the city's reserved exterior, one
that closely resembles the culture and values of the Institute.

Will's relationship with Annie Kate Gervais deepens the parallels between
Charleston and the Institute. Will first meets Annie Kate when she haughtily
chastises him for parking his car in her upscale neighborhood. He quickly realizes, however, that her snobbishness is a desperate performance and that Annie
Kate has only a tenuous hold on her place in society: she has become pregnant
by a well-connected young man who has refused to marry her, and both the
pregnancy and her presence in the city are a secret kept from all but a few
people. Her self-exile, which she must maintain until she can give the baby up
for adoption, is necessary in the unforgiving social climate of Charleston society: much like a cadet found guilty of an honor violation at the Institute, her
honor has been compromised, both by her sexual indiscretion and, as crucially,
by her failure to be accepted by her socially superior lover. If she is exposed,
she risks the humiliation and alienation of being drummed out of the society
that defines her.

Drawn in equal parts to her beauty, her vulnerability, and her quick cynicism, Will falls in love with Annie Kate, but the relationship is defined by a
willful blindness. Just as Will's roommate Dante Pignatti, known as Pig, is
seemingly unable to distinguish a meaningful difference between the image of
his girlfriend and her actual presence, beating up cadets who use vulgarity in
front of a photo of her, Will is invested in a version of Annie Kate that often
denies her true complexity. He associates her pregnancy with a form of mystic
maternal power, for instance, and her acceptance of him as fully transformative. He cements the fantasy of their relationship by imagining marrying Annie Kate and adopting her baby, thus restoring her honor. Will is shocked and
heartbroken, then, when Annie Kate cuts off all contact with him after she gives
birth to a stillborn child. Even as he has listened to her speak of her despair
during the isolation of her pregnancy, he has not fully acknowledged her deep
need to be reintegrated into the society from which she has feared expulsion.
Indeed when she breaks off her relationship with Will, she explains not only
that she does not want to maintain an association with anyone who shared her
painful period of exile, but also that "I can't ever love someone like you. We're
too different. . . . I want things you can never give me" (391). Annie Kate's
abrupt rejection of Will as a serious partner is certainly reflective of the shock
and self-doubt she is experiencing in the wake of her traumatic pregnancy and
birth experience, but it also speaks to her deep indoctrination in the strict values of aristocratic society.

Annie Kate's belief that she can return to Charleston society after her
pregnancy has been "erased" reveals her deep misunderstanding of the politics
of such a system, however; her pregnancy may not have been exposed, but her
perceived social transgressions are not as easily forgiven. Toward the close of
the novel, Will is shocked to learn that the boy "from a fine family" who has
impregnated and then abandoned her is Tradd, and almost every component
of the affair—its consummation, its conclusion, and, ultimately, its inclusion
of Will—is shaped not by personal passions but by social calculations (391).
For instance Tradd confesses to his roommates that he seduced Annie Kate,
who remains unnamed in the conversation, because he hoped sexual experience
might inoculate him from the taunts of the other cadets, who have nicknamed
him "the Honey Prince" and repeatedly call him a "faggot" (256). With some
dismay he reports that "nothing changed" (257), a fact that is true of his reputation within the corps but certainly does not reflect Annie Kate's experience.
For Annie Kate, of course, everything has changed, and her honor has been the
price of Tradd's attempt to establish his masculinity in a system that privileges
heteronormativity above all else.

Tellingly, however, Tradd himself does not end the relationship; instead when Abigail learns of the pregnancy, she intervenes, persuading Tradd that Annie Kate is trying to ensnare him in order to rise in Charleston society and that their union would hurt his status. (Annie Kate's father is from North Charleston, an area that is just a few miles from the mansions "South of Broad" yet exists on the other side of an untraversable social chasm.) Abigail then orchestrates a relationship between Will and Annie Kate as a means of ensuring that Annie Kate has a companion throughout her pregnancy, an act that she characterizes as sympathetic but that is certainly reflective of Machiavellian impulses as well: if Annie Kate is entertained, she will not be as tempted to call upon the St. Croixs for support. Regardless of her motives, Abigail's careful distancing of Annie Kate dooms her fate in Charleston society. Indeed Annie Kate later realizes that Tradd had been her "last chance," and as the novel closes she is living in California, pretending she is "a charming Southern belle from an aristocratic family," an imitation of the life she had hoped to lead (558). In aiding in Annie Kate's exile and in tricking Will into service as Tradd's emotional surrogate, Abigail demonstrates a deft understanding of the ways that power can be used in its own defense and that the notion of honor can be manipulated to preserve the status quo.

This lesson is repeated in equally dramatic form when Will and his roommates Pig and Mark learn that the Ten does indeed exist; dedicated to "preserv[ing] the purity and integrity of the Corps of Cadets" (315), a rhetoric that noticeably echoes that of the Ku Klux Klan, the Ten takes undesirable plebes who have survived conventional hazing and tortures them until they quit (315). Threatened with exposure, the members of the Ten engage in a campaign to run Will, Pig, and Mark out of the Institute, and the nerve-jarring standoff between the roommates and the Ten quickly dissolves into a feeling of inevitable defeat when they catch Pig siphoning gas from Will's car. (Pig has stolen the gas because he is loath to ask his roommates for more money, an act of pride that ironically is also an honor violation.) In a cascading series of events dictated by Institute protocol, Pig is placed under room arrest, tried and found guilty of stealing at a trial of the honor court, and summarily drummed out of school. This figurative death, in which all of the Institute's cadets turn their back on him, is followed by a literal one: Pig immediately places himself in the path of an oncoming train and is killed.

Pig's death reverberates throughout the novel. Pig, Will, Mark, and Tradd have been as close as brothers throughout their years at the Institute, and Will punctuates his narrative with rhapsodic accounts of their genuine and overwhelming love for one another. The roommates know each other in ways that no one else can: in enduring the same trials, and in recognizing one another as individuals in a system that prizes conformity, their lives are intimately intertwined. Even beyond this essential connection, the experience of exposing the Ten has brought Will, Mark, and Pig closer. In their quest to root out the Ten, they have unconsciously refined their construction of honor, often violating Institute rules in the service of what they recognize to be right: they kidnap Ten alumnus Daniel Molligen in order to extract information from him, for instance, and they sneak off campus to save Tom Pearce after he is splashed with gasoline and threatened with immolation in one of the Ten's torture sessions. Their already close bond deepens as they discover a shared brand of physical and moral bravery.

Yet when Pig is found guilty of committing an honor violation, the remaining roommates are paralyzed. While they have defended him before the honor court, after Pig has been condemned to expulsion they find themselves mechanically acting as they have been instructed, "putting distance between ourselves and him . . . [and] beginning the merciless process of turning him into a stranger" (490). Though Will later wishes they had joined Pig in his walk of shame, identifying their friendship as more intimate and meaningful than the fraternity of the corps, in that crucial moment, they quickly adopt the silence that is required of them. Even as they have reconsidered and reshaped their understanding of honor in their quest to bring down the Ten, they have no way of privileging personal honor over institutional honor. Just as Pig throws himself in front of the train in a desperate attempt to seek "one last moment of pride and honor" (495), his remaining roommates feel they have been left no good choices, and the idea of "honor" seems increasingly murky.

As Will and Mark seek to avenge Pig's death, the essential duplicity or integrity of a number of the novel's secondary characters is exposed. General Durrell, for example, always relatively contemptible in Will's eyes for his self-aggrandizing and preening manner, is revealed to be morally baseless, a Ten alumnus who actively facilitates the group's unimaginably brutal torture sessions. Conversely Colonel Berrineau, whom Will briefly had been led to believe was a member of the Ten, is confirmed to be fiercely ethical, directly confronting Durrell after Will comes to him with his findings and refusing to back down even when threatened with the loss of his career. Yet while Durrell and the Bear dramatically articulate antipodal approaches to honor, the novel is clearly more interested in the sort of equivocality that is evinced in Will's and Mark's helpless acceptance of Pig's dismissal, and it is through this lens that the actions of their fourth roommate, Tradd St. Croix, must be viewed. As critic Landon C. Burns has noted, Tradd is "the ultimate Judas in the novel," and the evidence of his betrayals is damning: in addition to abandoning Annie

Kate, he is exposed as a member of the Ten and thus has contributed directly to Pig's expulsion and indirectly to his death, and he undoubtedly would have aided in the plot to have Mark and Will expelled had the Ten not been exposed.[7] Yet as reprehensible as his actions are, Tradd is not a villain in the ilk of Durrell; instead he is driven by a need to belong that is rendered understandable, if not wholly sympathetic, throughout the novel. As the "Honey Prince," Tradd's masculinity, the most meaningful capital at the Institute, is always in question. When he is invited to join the Ten, he is not only being tapped for an exclusive place in the Institute's hierarchy; he is being invited to judge others' worthiness rather than to be judged mercilessly himself.

Had Tradd not tried to deny his own culpability in Pig's death when confronted, Will might have understood his position to some extent. Will, of course, sees his own responsibilities on the honor court, the sanctioned body of judgment, as central to his identity: the act of judgment reifies his own understanding of himself as honorable. Even more important, though, is the fact that throughout the novel Will repeatedly, if uncomfortably, recognizes his own need to have his moral authority recognized. Early in the novel, he acknowledges that "my goodness is my vanity, my evil" and that he is driven by "a genuine need to be my own greatest hero" (104). He recognizes this impulse as central in accepting his position as Pearce's ally, candidly confessing that "I was a natural to take care of Pearce, not because of my radiant humanity (although that is what I wanted to believe) but because he would be indebted to me and I could rule him and own him and even loathe him because I had made him a captive of my goodness" (104). Moreover when Pearce does not seem to be appropriately grateful for Will's help, deviating from the "atavistically Southern" (366) relationship they both recognize as existing between them, Will becomes surly, even telling Pearce that he is engaging in "nigger talk," as a way of subconsciously rebalancing the scales (371). This same need to be both powerful and righteous is manifested in his relationship with Annie Kate; he desires to "save" her through marriage not simply because of his genuine love for her but because of the deep appeal of the role of savior. In helping those who have been marginalized —Pearce by his race, Annie Kate by both her gender and her fragile class status—Will recognizes that he is able to affirm his own superiority.

Given Will's merciless self-assessment throughout the novel, it may be argued that his anger at Tradd not only is a response to Tradd's betrayal of Pig and Annie Kate but also is reflective of his all-too-intimate understanding of the ways in which the Institute encourages this sort of callow and cruel action. For instance when Will, Mark, and Pig kidnap Molligen, Will not only assists in tying Molligen to the train tracks in an attempt to trick him into thinking he will be crushed by a train, he also hits Molligen several times when he is tied up and defenseless. Later he admits to himself that "cruelty was an easy sport to master when practiced anonymously. I was shaking again, not from revulsion at what I had done, but from something more sinister. I was shaking because I had enjoyed it all so much, every bit of it. I had especially enjoyed slapping Molligen and making him bleed. It was as though I was striking out against everything that had ever hurt or frightened me" (422). Just as Tradd feels released from his role as the Honey Prince when he participates in one of the Ten's plots, a sense of relief so powerful that he is willing to ignore its consequences, Will acknowledges that he has felt empowered by an act of violence that might have sickened him had he witnessed another cadet committing it.

Similarly even as Will denounces Tradd for leaving Annie Kate when he knows she will be at her loneliest and most frightened in order to preserve the future he imagines for himself, Will also recognizes himself as having engaged in a form of parallel behavior, if on a much smaller scale. As the star of the Institute basketball team, Will has taken on hero status to the team's towel boy, Bo Maybank. Despite his undeniable talent and dedication, Bo is too short to play basketball at the college level, and he pours his frustrated energies into his support of Will: not only does he religiously attend to Will's needs, bringing him warm towels and giving him massages, but he also takes genuine joy in Will's successes on the court. When Will sinks a winning shot in overtime in the final game against VMI, Bo is eager to be a part of the moment, and Will recalls, "I remembered his tiny leaps up toward me after the VMI game and I regretted I had not looked down from the shoulders of my roommates, from the accolades of the crowd, looked down and done the right thing for once in my life, the grand and perfect gesture. I should have lifted Bo Maybank up with me, and together we should have taken that last frantic ride to the locker room. But I didn't; I wanted it all, all for myself" (364).

To share the experience would have been to cede some of the power of his rare moment of glory, and in this way Will's decision not to include Bo in his celebration is reflective of the same self-protective instinct that guides Tradd to allow his mother to orchestrate the exile of Annie Kate. The Institute has trained its cadets that they are to be either victors or victims, and they have been instructed from the beginning of their careers that they must not empathize with those rendered casualties of such thinking. This attitude is symbolized by an Institute tradition in which "each freshman must piss on the lion [in the Charleston zoo] before the beginning of the sophomore year," despite—or perhaps because of—the fact that "he was old and humiliated and smelled strongly of human urine" (236). The animal's plight suggests that people, too, can become degraded and discarded if they are identified as weak or wanting in some fashion: plebes are run out if they are deemed not strong enough; Bo

Maybank is ignored because he is not tall enough; and Annie Kate is abandoned because her background is not aristocratic enough. Such a system is inherently terrifying, and Tradd and Will, like their fellow cadets, are driven by a fear of exposing their own weaknesses.

Even as he is influenced by these truths, Will is haunted by them. As a result—unlike many of the cadets who internalize the Institute's value system, as Tradd ultimately does, or who follow its more questionable edicts along with those they find meaningful, as Pig and Mark do—from an early point in his career, Will finds himself resisting a system he identifies as soul killing. He upbraids himself not only when he fails to live up to his own code but also when he finds himself fitting in too neatly with the Institute's ethos, and he welcomes the voice of a "guerilla within," a rebellious secret identity that demands that Will "unlearn the system while [he] was still a part of it" (173, 174). As a result Will often experiences the desperate loneliness associated with any form of double consciousness: he explains that he "never felt lonelier than when [he] marched with the regiment, in step with the two thousand" (238). As much as he seeks to mark himself as out of step in some ways—by neglecting to wear his uniform according to Institute standards, for example, or, less visibly but more dramatically, by proclaiming a series of unpopular liberal views—in fact Will is also deeply troubled by his isolation, and while The Lords of Discipline is often identified as a "page turner" by many critics, the very human loneliness that saturates Will's tenure at the Institute is as powerful as the plot twists that drive the novel.

The great irony of Will's isolation—one that he suggests but never fully acknowledges—is that in the brutal systems typified by the Institute and Charleston society, almost everyone is made to feel like an outsider, even those whose credentials would suggest otherwise. Will's narration is filled with references to other characters' loneliness. He feels confident in first approaching Pig, for example, because he recognizes that "powerful men inspire fear, [and thus] they usually have very few friends . . . I knew with absolute surety that Pig had isolated and imprisoned himself in his own physical invulnerability. He was lonely that first year" (45). Tradd is similarly alienated by his *lack* of power, and Will remarks that he "was one of the most isolated people I had ever known, a boy of such deep essential silences and unvoiced questions I almost felt I had never met or touched him, but only observed him from a distance" (241). Likewise Edward Reynolds, a favored history professor who has spent a lifetime at the Institute and serves as its chief chronicler, is "a supremely lonely man" (310), and Annie Kate is pained by even the suggestion of abandonment, refusing to wave to the ships leaving Charleston Harbor, and at one point telling Will plaintively, "The loneliness is killing me" (267). The tragedy of such closed systems is that while there is real affection and genuine connection between these characters, they cannot address one another's loneliness. The realities of isolation are too terrifying to confront, and as a result, the characters in the novel exist in sympathy but fail to offer one another consolation.

The conclusion of the novel captures this alienation, as each of the narrative threads is resolved not through communion and fraternity but through a fragmentation of experience. For instance after Will, Mark, and the Bear expose and neutralize the Ten, Pearce essentially disappears from the narrative. Will and Pearce never claim a joint victory, nor do they reflect on their relationship. Shortly thereafter Will reveals to Tradd that he knows Tradd is both a member of the Ten and the father of Annie Kate's baby, and he bitterly breaks off his relationship with Tradd and the St. Croixs. In their final exchange, Tradd cries out to him, "Tell me you don't love me, Will," and Will replies perfunctorily, "I can't tell you that, Tradd" (555). Even though Will continues to feel connected to Tradd—and, to some extent, to see his own insecurities reflected in him—he believes that their friendship now comes at too high a price, and both men face their futures without the other. Similarly Annie Kate writes Will a letter at Abigail's behest, and while she provides some insight into her choices, she concludes her letter by asking Will not to contact her. Their relationship, like his connections to Pearce and Tradd, is fully severed. Even Mark, Will's remaining roommate, is essentially unavailable to him at the end of the novel. While Will and Mark have solidified their bond after the physical loss of Pig and the emotional loss of Tradd, they find that they celebrate their graduation not as intimates but with "the rest of the four hundred [cadets] (560)." Not long afterward Mark is killed in Vietnam.

Fittingly the final exchange of the novel is between Will and the Bear. Colonel Berrineau has served as an important symbol of personal integrity throughout the novel, and his steady presence amid the wreckage of the novel's conclusion is a reminder of Will's early idealism. With this understanding Will approaches the Bear after graduation and asks him to sign his diploma, telling him, "I want the name of a man I can respect on my diploma, Colonel." Without missing a beat, the Bear replies, "There already is," and points to Will's own name (561). In this simple yet gracious gesture, the Bear suggests that Will has attained manhood on his own terms, defining a code of honor that is in the spirit of the Institute even as it defies General Durrell's vision of it. While the Bear's valediction functions as a definitive and satisfying affirmation, though, the quietness of this moment stands in sharp contrast to the exuberance of the formal recognition of Will's manhood at the ring ceremony, which takes place at the center of the novel. The ring is the Institute's ultimate symbol of inclusion, and accordingly Will finds himself caught up in the ceremony in which it is awarded; putting all cynicism aside, he thrills in both the official sanction of his manhood and the idea of being "linked . . . to the Line, for as long as I lived" (299). When the Bear points to Will's name on his diploma, however, the sense of communion suggested by the ring ceremony evaporates; Berrineau's gesture is, in fact, a confirmation of Will's observation that "though I wore the ring, I was not one of them" (560). In this way the novel's final scene underscores the essential solitude of Will's position, and it reinforces the bittersweet tinge to the novel's opening line: "I wear the ring" (1). For Will the ambivalence that defines much of the novel will never be resolved, and his relationship with the Institute will always be an uneasy one.

While *The Lords of Discipline*'s exploration of masculine honor shapes almost all of its characters, the novel also addresses and expands upon a number of themes that are central to Conroy's larger oeuvre. Most significantly, perhaps, the role of women, and mothers in particular, undergoes a dramatic shift in this novel. In *The Great Santini* Lillian Meecham is a flawed model of belledom, but her beauty and graciousness continue to dominate Ben's understanding of her. In the opening pages of *The Lords of Discipline*, however, Will concedes that his mother often defies his understanding, confessing that he is "always writing revisionist histories" of herself (5). Significantly he acknowledges that while he has enrolled in the Institute because of a promise made to his father, this vow has been enforced by his mother, a fact neither Will nor his mother acknowledge in service of the myth of his paternal obligation. Even more obviously, we see Abigail St. Croix as a formidable figure; beneath her warm, maternal exterior, she is as strategically adept and morally corrupt as General Durrell. Annie Kate's mother lacks Abigail's power, but she is just as guided by a desire to maintain appearances: after Annie Kate has failed to marry a man who will provide social and economic security for them both, Mrs. Gervais is regularly drunk and often seems incapable of basic kindness. Even Annie Kate herself suggests the damage that mothers may inflict on their children, both in her reluctance to connect with the baby that is growing inside her despite Will's prodding, and in the fact that when it is born, the child is dead, symbolically strangled by its umbilical cord. As Conroy's work develops, the figure of the mother becomes increasingly complex, and the origins of this transformation are evident in *The Lords of Discipline,* a novel ostensibly concerned with paternalistic authority.

Sex is also treated more broadly in *The Lords of Discipline.* In *The Great Santini,* sex is always couched in the language of shame: Ben's Catholic upbringing has made him squeamish about any acknowledgement of sex, and Mary Anne regularly dismisses the attraction between her parents as "sicko-sexual." In *The Lords of Discipline,* Catholicism still shapes Will's

understanding of sex; even after he and Annie Kate consummate their relationship, he believes that sex "was some grotesque and beastly urge of men
that women endured as part of the misery of their station" (367). Will is also
influenced by his residency on an all-male campus, however, where stories of
sexual conquest—or its opposite, frequent masturbation—abound. Moreover
he recognizes the erotic undertones of homosocial military culture, evident in
everything from the close-fitting uniforms to formations in which cadets stand
in pantomimes of physical intimacy. In such a culture, sexual potency is linked
with manhood, and the shame Will has been taught to associate with sex is
overshadowed by a celebration of its role within a construction of military
masculinity. In Conroy's later novels, the male protagonists continue to wrestle
with the competing impulses of shame and pleasure, particularly as they are
involved in meaningful long-term adult relationships.

As was true of each of Conroy's previous books, the publication of *The
Lords of Discipline* was met with controversy, although this time the "family"
Conroy had angered was the Citadel: the school quickly banned the novel—and
Conroy—from its campus.[8] (Interestingly Conroy foreshadows this controversy
in the novel itself in that texts repeatedly place their authors in peril: Will's
poem about upperclassmen earns him a beating that would have broken him
had not he been saved by a fellow basketball player, for instance, and Com-
merce St. Croix's journals provide clues that expose the membership of the
Ten, Tradd's betrayal of Annie Kate, and, more incidentally, his own infideli-
ties.) This rupture with his alma mater was made more dramatic in 1995 when
Conroy supported the admission of Shannon Faulkner, the first female cadet
to the Citadel, actively pushing for the sort of diversification he depicts in *The
Lords of Discipline*. The schism was resolved, in part, after the release of *My
Losing Season,* Conroy's memoir of his senior year on the Citadel basketball
team, a work that is discussed in chapter 7.[9]

If the Citadel was outraged by the novel, the public was fascinated, however,
and it quickly became a bestseller and, like each of Conroy's previous books,
was adapted for film, this time directed by Franc Roddam and starring David
Keith. The novel also garnered good reviews in the national press, solidifying
Conroy's reputation as a compelling storyteller and an effective chronicler
of his age. Writing for the *Washington Post Book World,* for example, Frank
Rose articulated a view characteristic of many reviews when he wrote that *The
Lords of Discipline* gives its reader a clear sense of "the terrible price that any
form of manhood can extract." "Conroy's personal triumph," he added, "is in
conveying all this in a novel that practically quivers with excitement and conviction."[10] Writer Harry Crews contributed a more mixed review to the *New
York Times Book Review*. Crews praised the extended flashback at the heart of

the book that looks at Will's plebe year, crediting Conroy with "lay[ing] open the barbaric nature of the human heart," but took issue with the plot turns in the second half of the book, suggesting that Conroy's "creative energies are sidetracked" by "clever puzzles."[11] This charge is one that would follow Conroy throughout his career as his fiction developed even more dramatic plotlines, beginning with his next novel, the work with which Conroy is most closely associated, *The Prince of Tides.*

CHAPTER 5

The Prince of Tides

The six years between the publication of *The Lords of Discipline* and *The Prince of Tides* (1986) were marked by a number of important shifts in Pat Conroy's life. Professionally Conroy found a new sense of stability when he began working with celebrated editor Nan Talese midway through the writing of *The Prince of Tides;* after working with a different editor for each of his previous books, Conroy settled into a comfortable relationship with Talese that continued to shape his career in the ensuing decades.[1] Conroy's personal life, on the other hand, was in the process of profound change. In 1981 he wed Lenore Gurewitz Fleischer, a divorcée with two teenaged children, Gregory and Emily. The marriage was quickly infected by the bitterness of Fleischer's battles with her ex-husband, the most serious of which were focused on Emily's accusations that her father had sexually molested her. Conroy immediately took on a role as Emily's advocate, but the reality of her suffering as well as the emotional and financial costs of the extended, and often ugly, legal battles with Alan Fleischer left Conroy exhausted and depressed. He relocated his family to Rome as a way of escaping what was becoming a toxic environment in Atlanta.

The Conroys added another daughter to the family, Susannah, in the first year of their marriage, and the blended family lived in Rome for almost three years, after which Conroy returned to the South to be closer to his mother, who was dying of leukemia. His 1995 novel *Beach Music* draws from his experiences during this period, depicting both his deep love of Rome and the enormous difficulty of Peggy Conroy's death, but in the years he lived in Italy, Conroy's work was firmly rooted in the South: "When I was in Rome I wrote a great deal of *Prince of Tides*—I could see Beaufort, perfectly, and I missed it."[2] The remove from the South afforded Conroy a chance to think about southern experience more expansively, and thus while the evidence of his personal history is still imprinted upon the novel, particularly in its depiction of protagonist Tom Wingo's parents, Henry and Lila, who are again modeled after Don and Peggy Conroy, *The Prince of Tides* also offers a more fully articulated vision of post-modern southern identity than is evinced in his previous novels. The themes that Conroy touches on in his earlier work—masculinity, racial privilege, physical and psychic violence, faith, and home—are probed in new depth here. Moreover in his creation of Tom Wingo, Conroy subtly shifts the voice of what has become an identifiable Conroy hero; Tom's identity as a middle-aged man coming to terms with his own failures deviates from the more earnest outrage associated with Conroy's adolescent characters, and the novel is imbued with a sense of melancholia that has its roots in the work of Walker Percy or William Styron as much as it does the novels of Thomas Wolfe.

To sum up the plot of *The Prince of Tides* is a daunting task: as Conroy's former editor Jonathan Galassi wrote in an admiring letter, "the book has enough in it for ten ordinary novels."[3] The story focuses on the Wingo children—Luke and twins Savannah and Tom—whose childhood is steeped in the pleasures of their own close-knit connection and the beauty of the South Carolina lowcountry and, at the same time, is shaped by a sense of pervasive fear and lingering despair. Like *The Great Santini*'s Bull Meecham, Henry Wingo beats his wife and children, but in *The Prince of Tides* this violence quickly is reduced to a backdrop against which unimaginable acts of violation take place: over the course of their adolescence, the Wingo siblings are affected by a series of terrifying acts of stalking, rape, and murder. The stories of the Wingos' upbringing are revealed over the course of a summer when Tom, now in his late thirties, travels to New York to work with Susan Lowenstein, the therapist who is trying to restore Savannah from the fugue state she has entered after her most recent suicide attempt. The novel is propelled by the tension between the past, which Tom shares with Lowenstein in a fragmented fashion, and the present, in which Tom must come to terms with his own failures and address his evolving relationship with Lowenstein. These twin threads build upon one another as the explosive revelations of the past empower Tom to move forward in the present, and ultimately the novel represents the full maturation of both Conroy's style and thematic focus.

Like Conroy's previous work, *The Prince of Tides* is preoccupied with notions of southern manhood, but if the protagonists of *The Great Santini* and *The Lords of Discipline* are worried about the ways in which they might not measure up to the standards that have been set for them, Tom Wingo is painfully aware of the ways he has already failed. As the novel opens, he has been fired from his position as a football coach, an event that emasculates him in that it situates his wife, Sallie, as the breadwinner of the family and that it robs him of his identity as a coach, removing him from the fraternity of the playing field.[4] Tom's lack of sexual desire is further evidence of his unmanning: early in the novel, he confesses that "my body had not felt like an instrument of love or passion for such a long time" (25), and when Sallie tells him she is having an affair, Tom sees it as an inevitability as much as it is a betrayal. Indeed he views the failure of his marriage as part of a larger pattern, noting that he disappoints "all the women who loved me" by "turning them slowly and by degrees from lovers into friends" (350). Tom is not asexual—indeed he describes a lively fantasy life—and as a football player and coach, he is certainly familiar with the conventions of performative masculinity, but throughout the novel he rejects the posture of the virile southern man, retreating to an image of himself as a "completely defeated male . . . neutered by life and circumstances" (448).

Shame in his impotence—his inability to act in the assigned role of the southern man—is one of the defining characteristics of Tom's identity and one of the most prominent themes of *The Prince of Tides*. Even as a child, Tom repeatedly feels as if he fails the tests that would affirm his manhood, and he is haunted by his own tendency toward inaction and the feelings of disgrace that follow. He is unable to protect his mother, Lila, from his father's beatings, standing by helplessly even as his siblings try to intervene, and this failure is echoed and inflated when Lila is stalked by a terrifying man the children call "Callanwolde," the name of the woods from which he first appears. Callanwolde's appearance during the period the family has relocated to Atlanta when Henry is at war suggests his function as Henry's nightmarish surrogate; his grossly exaggerated physicality and monstrous sexuality are amplifications of the threat that Henry poses to his family and are a perversion of the sort of manhood to which Tom aspires. It is telling, then, that every time Callanwolde approaches Lila, Tom is frozen in place. When Callanwolde first attempts to break into the house, his exposed phallus underscoring his intentions, the family jumps into action: Savannah screams, Luke attacks him with a fireplace poker, Lila calls the police, and Tolitha, Lila's mother-in-law, shoots at him with a revolver. Tom alone is paralyzed, feeling as inert as "a Novocained gum" (132–33). His response is understandable; indeed given the fact that all of the children are under the age of ten, it is his siblings' immediate action that may be more remarkable. Yet Tom's inability to act, or even to speak of the attack in its aftermath, leads him to see himself as "pathetic," in his own word (133).

Tom remains mute for two full days after the attack, incapable of processing the terrifying combination of violence, sex, and power he has just witnessed. His silence also links him to a distinctly liminal masculinity: Papa John, Tolitha's ailing husband, has slept through the attack, and Tolitha and Lila, accepting "southern women['s] . . . responsibility to protect their men from danger and bad news," do not tell him about it (133). Tom has figuratively slept through the attack, and his silence—an inability to come to terms with "bad news"—further aligns him with the infirm Papa John. If Luke, who instinctively grabs a fireplace poker when he spots Callanwolde, represents an idealized manhood, Papa John and Tom embody a form of manhood that has been evacuated of authority and, equally significant, is dependent upon the strength of women to protect and buttress it.

Callanwolde attacks the family a second time while they are in Atlanta, and in this instance Luke and Savannah repel him by throwing Papa John's collection of black widow spiders at him while, once again, Tom is frozen in place. This second bout of paralysis deepens Tom's sense of shame, and it prefigures the ways in which he is unable to act when, ten years later, Callanwolde and two other convicts track Lila down after the family has returned to their home on remote Melrose Island. In the most devastating scene in the novel—and among the most brutal in Conroy's oeuvre—Lila, Savannah, and Tom are raped by the three criminals, and Tom, now eighteen, is fully emasculated through his inability to aid his mother and sister, who "[call] out [his] name, begging for [his] intercession" during the assault, and through his own rape and near-castration (491). The rapes are interrupted when Luke barges onto the scene and, employing a tiger that Henry had acquired in a get-rich-quick scheme, kills Callanwolde. Luke's appearance also allows Tom and Savannah to act, killing their attackers, but there is little comfort for either. As Tom later thinks to himself, "Though our bodies would heal, our souls had sustained a damage beyond compensation" (495).

As was the case after Callanwolde's first attack, Tom's inability to act during the assault is followed by a damning silence. In this case, however, his silence is externally imposed: Lila insists that the children tell no one about the rapes and murders. As Tom notes, this decision is "crazy. It's nuts. It's sick" (498). Yet Lila's suppression of the assault is also in keeping with her stoic construction of southern womanhood; above all else she desires to protect herself from the town's gossip and Henry's rejection and to ensure that Savannah is seen as a virgin by eligible men. The magnitude of the family's secret causes Savannah to attempt suicide for the first time, and Tom is also set adrift, albeit in in less obvious ways. Lila has not simply suppressed the fact of his rape but fully erased it, insisting, "A man cannot be raped by another man" (496). Already alienated from the model of manhood embodied by Luke's instinctive bravery, Tom finds himself divorced from his mother and sister's experience through Lila's expurgation of his trauma. Thus the encounters with Callanwolde—and the crucial silences that follow—leave him feeling emasculated and, as important, intimidated by a form of female power that he identifies as both defining and damaging.

Notably *The Prince of Tides* engages in a much more complex consideration of female identity than is evident in Conroy's previous work, and the novel is populated by a number of fully developed female characters beyond the central figure of Susan Lowenstein, Savannah's urbane, Jewish psychiatrist. Tolitha Wingo, for example, is a character who might easily have been reduced to a role as one of the charismatic eccentrics who fill out the novel, yet her unrepentant embrace of her controversial history elevates her within the narrative. Her decision to leave her first husband, Amos, and young Henry during the Depression in order to recast her own fate, and her continued refusal to make choices that cede to social expectations—including her multiple marriages and even her eventual return to Amos—make Tolitha an extraordinary model of female autonomy. Similarly Savannah privileges the independent self over the conventions of southern womanhood. In her fierce intellect and unconventional bravery, she exists in the mode of *The Great Santini*'s Mary Anne Meecham, and while Savannah is perhaps even more deeply damaged by her family, unlike Mary Anne she has found a voice—and an audience—through poetry.[5]

Yet it is Lila, a woman who hews closely to the model of the southern belle, who remains the richest female character in the novel and whose presence is felt in all of Tom's relationships with women. Like *The Great Santini*'s Lillian Meecham, Lila is recognizable as a classic "steel magnolia," a woman whose cultivated beauty and performative passivity mask a formidable strength, but she is also shaped by a sense of desperation that becomes more visible with the passage of time. Made deeply unhappy by both her marriage and her inferior social position, Lila engages in a continual assessment of her options and views the world around her with a calculating eye. Shortly after she gives birth to her fourth stillborn child, for example, she recognizes that her family will not grow beyond its current configuration and seeks to reinforce perceived alliances with her existing children. Lila approaches each child, unbeknownst to the others, and confesses, "I've only got you. . . . I don't have anyone else. It's going to be all up to you," insisting that the other two children are too deeply flawed to assist her or carry on her legacy (180). Lila's cunning is laid bare here, and the entreaty she makes captures the ways in which she functions as an adoring mother to each of her children and at the same time is willing to manipulate them to her own ends.

Lila becomes an object of preoccupation for Tom, and he is constantly shifting in his assessment of her, a fact that is signaled in the sharp contrast between the prologue, in which Lila is seen as "a beautiful, word-struck" woman who can "call forth" the moon for her children in a performance that sparkles with magic (6), and the first chapter, in which her remoteness is captured in her insistence that she cannot go to New York in the wake of Savannah's suicide attempt because she is "giving a dinner party Saturday night and it's been planned for months" (21). Tom finds himself caught between his childhood adulation of Lila and his contempt for her as an adult, and consequently their relationship remains perpetually destabilizing for him. Lila becomes an undeciphered Rosetta Stone, and Tom believes that "since I failed to know my mother, I was denied the gift of knowing the other women who would cross my path" (112). Yet Tom not only attributes to his mother his inability to connect authentically with women; he also believes that he seeks to replicate their relationship in a way that condemns him to employ women as a tool in an ongoing act of self-emasculation. In a particularly bitter observation, for example, he attributes many of the failures of his marriage to Sallie to his unresolved relationship with Lila, noting, "In Sallie, I had formed the woman who would be a subtle, more cunning version of my own mother. Like my mother, my wife had come to feel slightly ashamed of and disappointed in me. The configuration and tenor of my weakness would define the fury of their resurrection; my failure would frame their strength, blossoming, and deliverance" (103). In this vision Tom is doomed to reproduce his history by choosing women—or, as his rhetoric here suggests, *creating* women—who not only find him unworthy but also become increasingly powerful in the vacuum of his failed manhood.

Just as Tom conflates Sallie and Lila here, he repeatedly collapses the mother and lover roles, often adopting language that is naked in its Oedipal ideation. (In one reflection, for example, he contends that "there is nothing more erotic on earth than a boy in love with the shape and touch of his mother" [112].) Tom's unself-conscious acceptance of Freudian models, taken with the sort of casually misogynistic mockery inherent in his characterization of Savannah's fans as "a grim phalanx of women-warriors" who "looked as if they spent their time translating Sappho and drinking the blood of flies" (37) might suggest that Tom is, as he puts it, a typical "white southern male" (167), with all of the unchallenged privilege such a label implies. Yet he also self-identifies as a feminist, a claim that is central to his understanding of women and of himself. Admittedly he is highly skeptical of feminism as a movement; instead he embraces feminism as an ideology that recognizes the commonality of human experience and contributes to the erasure of conventional gender roles. This attitude is evinced in his enthusiastic support of, and genuine pride in, Sallie's medical career, for example, and in his swift and dismissive response when Lowenstein identifies Savannah's poetry as "written for and about women." Tom argues that such an identification "cheapens [Savannah's] work" (166), and he posits that the claim's latent essentialism is equally damaging to the male readership it excludes. For Tom feminism is a component of a liberal perspective that not only reframes the power of the marginalized but also allows for a more fluid definition of male identity.

In fact while Tom's feminism is rooted in a sincere rejection of the hierarchies that oppress women, it is equally reflective of his frustration with a construction of white, southern manhood that he finds more constricting than empowering. Tom tells Lowenstein, "[A] man who calls himself a feminist is the most ridiculous figure of our silly times. When I say it to my men friends, they chuckle and tell me the latest pussy joke. When I say it to most southern women, they look at me with utter contempt and say how much they enjoy being women and having car doors opened for them. When I say it to feminists, they are the most vicious of all. Feminists take it as an unctuous, patronizing gesture coming from some hairy spy planted by the enemy camp" (449). Tom's desire to cross ideological boundaries is seen a violation, one that threatens the strict formulations of identity that define southern society, and it leaves him feeling isolated and trapped. He tells Lowenstein that "I'm so sick of being strong, supportive, wise, and kingly that I may puke if I have to pretend I'm any of those things again" (450), and while she quickly and effectively identifies his compliant as overly simplistic, Tom's comment does reflect his very genuine feeling that he is imprisoned by a definition of masculinity that cannot accommodate his experiences and attitudes. His brand of feminism, then, is less an endorsement of the politics of his age than it is a reflection of his desire to recognize and to challenge tentatively the gendered boundaries that proscribe his identity.[6]

Tom's identity as a white southern male is further complicated by the fact that he is also a Catholic, and faith becomes an important theme in the novel, one that runs parallel to Conroy's treatment of masculinity. In *The Great Santini* and *The Lords of Discipline,* Conroy largely employs Catholicism as a way of underscoring his protagonists' feelings of isolation during their adolescence, and certainly Tom is aware of the relative "strangeness" of his religion in the Protestant South (170).[7] But the Catholicism depicted in this novel is not the monolithic faith that appears in Conroy's earlier work but, rather, an often paradoxical product of the Wingos' own creation. Lila and Henry convert to Catholicism after a German priest saves Henry when his plane is shot down in World War II. They have little guidance as they approach their new faith, and while, as Tom contends, they "brought a scrupulous obstinacy to their efforts to become the first practicing papists along their stretch of the Atlantic seaboard" (170), the dogma they embrace is reflective of their often uneven understanding of Catholic doctrine. As a result the Wingos' faith provides little succor, and indeed Catholicism is associated most closely with violence and transgression in the novel: for example just days after Henry first takes communion, he kills a pregnant woman to avoid detection as he tries to escape the Nazis; the priest who baptized Henry is killed by the Nazis when they learn that he sheltered the downed pilot; the only Catholic icon the family owns, a statue of the Infant of Prague, is one that Henry has stolen; and Tom uses this same statue to bludgeon his rapist after Callanwolde's last attack.

The novel features one truly religious character, Tolitha's husband, Amos, a retired Bible salesman who carries a cross down the main street of the Wingos' hometown of Colleton, South Carolina, every Good Friday in a reenactment of Christ's suffering. The ritual embarrasses Tom throughout his childhood, but as an adult he finds himself wishing that he had been more like his grandfather, noting that "I would like to have seen the world with eyes incapable of anything but wonder, and with a tongue fluent only in praise" (331). Yet Amos's faith is generally depicted in comic terms throughout the novel, and it remains a perplexing mix of sainthood and spectacle. He recounts his visions of God, in which God often shares his own worldview, in long letters to the editor of the local paper, for example, and during his Good Friday march, he develops an exaggerated stagger and often falls intentionally, because it "surprised the crowd" (336). As a sympathetic narrator, Tom makes it easy to appreciate the quirky nature of Amos's faith, but the power of his Good Friday walk is uncomfortably undercut in a scene in which Amos water-skis for forty miles in an act designed to inspire the return of his revoked driver's license. While each feat is remarkable in its demonstration of Amos's sincerity and determination, the parallels between these performances suggest that they are informed by a similar sense of folly. Amos's faith, certainly, is real, but like the Wingos' construction of Catholicism, it is so arbitrarily fashioned that it ultimately resigns him to a role as a "jester of burning faith" (331).

Surprisingly it is Luke Wingo who is able to adapt both the lessons of manhood that have frustrated Tom and the faith that has distorted Amos, and to assemble them in a way that is meaningful. Luke is a quiet figure in the first two-thirds of the novel, in part because Tom is unprepared to talk about him in his early conversations with Lowenstein and, in part, because for much of his life Luke occupies a diminished role in the family's consciousness. Regularly dismissed as the "stupid" child—a fact that is later belied by his IQ score—Luke's good-naturedness makes him less interesting in the eyes of his family members, each of whom are keenly aware of their own frustrated aspirations: Henry imagines himself to be an entrepreneur-in-the-making instead of a shrimper; Lila is desperate for the acceptance of the wealthier families of Colleton; Savannah is focused on leaving the South and becoming a writer; and Tom seeks to create the stable family he was deprived of as a child. Unlike the rest of the Wingos, whose restlessness is often a painful curse, Luke seems content to stay put—socially, economically, and geographically—and he happily follows Henry into shrimping.

Yet it is not any perceived shortcoming of intellect or ambition that keeps Luke home; more than any of the other characters in the novel, he feels a deep sense of place, and it is this authentic connection that grounds him in Colleton. As he has in his previous novels, Conroy paints an evocative picture of the South Carolina lowcountry in *The Prince of Tides,* indelibly mapping its geographic boundaries as well as its psychological borders. Yet here the landscape becomes increasingly meaningful: in *The Great Santini,* Ravenel's lushness represents a potential home for Ben Meecham, but he is also regularly reminded of its foreignness; and in *The Lords of Discipline,* Will McLean is enchanted with Charleston's beauty but is permanently excluded from its culture. For Luke, however, Colleton County and, more specifically, Melrose Island are home, and they are imbued with an almost mythic power in his eyes. While the Wingos' position as landowners may be suspect—Henry's great-grandfather won Melrose Island in a horseshoe game—Luke sees their island and the surrounding county as a crucible of familial and regional identity, a discrete space where the past is felt and tradition is embodied. Even as a child, he is not only at home in this landscape but also protective of it: when, in return for a substantial bounty, Henry helps a team from a Miami aquarium capture Snow, the beloved albino porpoise who frequents Colleton Sound, it is Luke who not only gives voice to the community's collective outrage but also orchestrates Snow's rescue and return. When he first discovers Henry's perfidy, Luke admonishes his father, "You don't sell what you can't replace" (364), and in returning Snow to the waters off Colleton, Luke is not only saving the animal but expressing an essential faith.

Ironically, though, it is not Henry who ultimately poses the biggest threat to the Wingo home but Lila. After threatening to leave Henry for years, she finally decides to divorce him after the children are grown. The move is a surprise to some extent—in his middle age, Henry has become a figure of pathos rather than terror —but it is soon apparent that Lila is not simply escaping her bad marriage but stepping into a new one.[8] When her former nemesis, Isabel Newbury, is diagnosed with cancer, Lila tends to her faithfully and is rewarded with an unconventional prize: Isabel decides that Lila should marry her husband, Reese, after her death. The marriage represents all that Lila has desired for herself: Reese is prepared to lavish attention on her, and more important, her new identity as a Newbury elevates Lila in society. Yet the marriage strikes her children as uncomfortable, not only in its pragmatic origins but in Lila's broader willingness to align herself with the Newburys, a clear betrayal of her own family's history.

The Newburys have wielded their status as a weapon for years, inflicting Lila with a stinging pain when Isabel pointedly bars her entry to the local women's club, for example, and frightening and shaming Tom when, in a particularly appalling move, Reese hits him after Tom has bested his son in a schoolyard fight. Indeed one of the greatest acts of family solidarity in the novel occurs when the Wingo children put a dead loggerhead turtle in Isabel and Reese's bed while the Newburys are on vacation. It is an act of wonderfully poetic justice; the turtle's decomposing corpse serves as a condemnation of the rotten faith that Isabel has demonstrated to Lila. Given this history, Lila's remarriage to Reese is not just a "spectacular break with the past" (557) but an unsettling of the Wingos' understanding of family and home.

Yet the marriage itself is just the first step in Lila's destabilization of home; indeed her union with Reese leads to the literal dismantling of the Wingo house and the decimation of their island. For years Reese has been buying property throughout Colleton County, and he has been stubbornly rebuffed by Henry in his attempts to purchase Melrose Island. When Lila leaves Henry, however, Reese manipulates their divorce settlement, ensuring that the island is awarded to Lila, despite the fact that she does not "care a single thing for that island" (599). After their marriage, Reese is able to bundle Melrose Island with his other properties and sell the entire county to the federal government so that it can be converted into a plutonium production site. The consequences of Lila's actions quickly reverberate through the community, both in their immediate realities and their symbolic iterations. For example the federal government relocates Colleton residents' houses to new communities, loading them on to river barges and floating them to their new destinations in a literal performance of the ways Colletonians have been sold down the river. Moreover, in making way for the production of plutonium, Lila has literally weaponized the Wingos' home place, a fact that metaphorically manifests itself in Luke's transformation into a guerrilla in a one-man war to defend his home.

Luke's battle for Colleton, which ends in his death, is the central trauma of Tom's adulthood, triggering his nervous breakdown and, presumably, Savannah's slide into psychosis. His already overwhelming grief becomes magnified, in part, because Luke's stand against the plutonium plant is an amalgam of the ideals of manhood and faith that have taunted Tom throughout his life. Luke, we learn, served with honor as a Navy SEAL in Vietnam, and his wartime experience only reinforced both his instinctive tendency toward action and his deep investment in the "sublimity of the southern way" (657). When Colleton is annexed, he immediately applies his SEAL skills to a cause that strikes him as righteous: in his vision plutonium represents an apocalypse, and the annexing of Colleton is akin to the loss of Eden. His decision to remain in Colleton and destroy equipment used in the conversion of the town to a plutonium factory is an articulation of the fierce faith Amos has typified, and his death at the hand of a government-supported sniper is an act of true martyrdom.[9]

As a result Tom's loss of his brother is accompanied by a sense that he has lost his own way as well. As the novel's famous opening line—"My wound is geography"—suggests, he shares Luke's connection to place, but he lacks Luke's conviction. As he tells Savannah just before Luke's death, "Luke has proven something to me. I'm not a man of principle, I'm not a man of faith, and I'm not a man of action. I have the soul of a collaborator. . . . I've become exactly the kind of man I hate more than anything in the world" (639). Tom's self-assessment, like that of Conroy's earlier characters, is often unduly harsh, but in the wake of Luke's death, he finds himself in a moment of true crisis. His manhood feels hollow to him, and he finally gives in to a complete breakdown, from which he emerges even more resigned to his self-perceived mediocrity. Tom is haunted by the traumas of his history and his failures to respond to them as he had once imagined he would, and as he tells Lowenstein, he has come to believe that "the worst is ahead of you because now you know the horror of the past. Now you know you have to live the memory of your fate and your history for the rest of your life. It is the Great Sadness and you know that it's your destiny" (348).

The "Great Sadness" Tom describes, in which memory and mourning are inseparably linked, threatens all of the Wingos. In order to stave off its inherent pain, they have been engaged in a collective struggle to deny the past: while Lila is most obvious in her reluctance to confront her history—Savannah wryly makes reference to "the old Mom technique. . . . Truth is only what you choose to remember" (638)—in fact all of the Wingos, save Luke, find themselves trying to escape its reach. Henry legitimately seems to have no recollection of beating his family, for instance, and Savannah's mental illness keeps her from remembering events even immediately after they have happened. Tom is the sanctioned vessel of the twins' collective memories, but he approaches the past only when he believes it is necessary to save Savannah, and even then he often qualifies his accounts with observations such as "I am more fabulist than historian" (77) and "My sister calls me the Coach of Unremembrance" (69).

Yet through his sessions with Lowenstein, Tom ultimately is compelled to come to terms with his past. While he presumably shares his stories in order to aid in Savannah's treatment, the unexpectedly plaintive cry he utters in his first meeting with Lowenstein, "Help *me*" (71), makes it clear that he understands that confronting the past is necessary for his own rehabilitation as well. Indeed the novel's present-day narrative functions as testimony to the ways in which Tom recovers essential elements of himself even as he is simultaneously chronicling his collapse in his conversations with Lowenstein: in teaching her son, Bernard, to play football, for instance, Tom reconnects with a part of his identity that is deeply meaningful to him, and most significantly, in his affair with Lowenstein, he is able to reclaim his emotional and sexual potency. Their affair infuses the novel with an optimism that the novel's plot might otherwise belie: there is a narrative satisfaction to their romance, of course, but their developing love for one another also signals the potential for deep and meaningful renewal. In her sessions with Tom, Lowenstein has demonstrated herself to be a gifted professional, guiding him as he revisits his most painful memories; in their romantic relationship, however, they instinctively "tell each other everything in the world" (665), accepting and absolving one another in a mutual spirit of love and generosity. It is through this relationship that Tom experiences "the return of hope and a clearance of all storm warnings in the danger zones of memory" (663).

As Tom comes to terms with his past, however, he must also make decisions about his future, choosing to remain with Lowenstein or to return to Sallie. Readers are given little insight into this decision, and when it is clear that Tom will return to his family in South Carolina, his choice seems at first to be further evidence of "the soul of a collaborator" that Tom has identified in himself. Certainly it is the less controversial path, and Tom acknowledges to Lowenstein that "if I were a braver man I could [stay with her]" (671). Yet he also tells her that he is returning to Sallie because "I chose to honor my own history" (671). In this assertion Tom identifies the ways in which their conversations—and indeed their relationship—have allowed him effectively to recuperate the past and illuminate his need to "make something beautiful out of the ruins" (672).

The novel ends with both the reconciliation of Tom and Sallie and a truce between Tom, Savannah, Lila, and Henry. Despite the tentativeness of their overtures to one another, a sense of sanguinity is injected into the family reunion when Sallie reenacts Lila's calling forth of the moon, a moment that Tom identifies in the novel's prologue as among the most magical of his childhood. Savannah in particular takes comfort in the both the natural and familial cycles evident in the performance, and after witnessing it she says, "Wholeness, Tom. It all comes back. It's all a circle" (678), suggesting that she and the other Wingos may find peace. Yet as he has in each of his previous novels, even as Conroy creates satisfying resolutions for each of the plot lines in *The Prince of Tides,* he simultaneously undermines the sense of stability they suggest, in this case with an overt nod: Tom's voice returns in the wake of the family's happy gathering, and he notes, "That should be the end of it, but it is not" (678). He then confesses that while he believes the choice he made is in keeping with "my real life, my destiny" (679), he continues to be pained by an image of the life with Lowenstein that he has sacrificed, and the novel ends as he repeats her name in a haunting incantation. The novel's final paragraphs suggest that no choice is without consequence and indeed that the "wholeness" that Savannah identifies as defining their lives may be as much an illusion as the act of calling forth the moon.

Almost immediately upon its release, *The Prince of Tides* was a legitimate sensation: it appeared for almost a full year on the hardback best-seller list and for another year after its paperback edition; it was made into a movie directed by and starring Barbra Streisand, which was nominated for seven Oscars, among other awards, including one for Conroy's work as a screenwriter; and it even was proposed as the basis for a television series, a plan that ultimately did not come to fruition.[10] Many reviews were overwhelming in their praise: Judy Bass, writing in the *Chicago Tribune,* for example, called *The Prince of Tides* a "brilliant novel that ultimately affirms life, hope, and the belief that one's future need not be contaminated by a monstrous past," and a review in the *Library Journal* praised Conroy for writing "a penetrating vision of the Southern psyche in this enormous novel of power and emotion."[11]

As they had since *The Water Is Wide,* though, a number of reviewers also took issue with Conroy's elaborate prose and dramatic plot twists. In the *New York Times Book Review,* for example, the novelist Gail Godwin suggested that "readers who have a high tolerance for the implausible, the sentimental and the florid will happily pad off to bed for a week or so with this hefty tale."[12] Conroy has never directly addressed these reviews—indeed he insists he has not read reviews of his work after feeling injured by them early in his career—but in an interview about the film adaptation of the novel, he acknowledged that "there's something about my writing that's a little overdone, even to me."[13] On the other hand, he seems perplexed by accusations of implausibility in his plots. Just as he can point to individuals who have inspired most of his characters, even minor ones, Conroy has explained that the majority of his work's gothic and fantastic elements are grounded in lived experience: in *The Prince of Tides* specifically, he has explained, Callanwolde is based on a man who stalked Peggy Conroy when she lived in Atlanta; Snow is a version of a porpoise who was regularly around Beaufort; the Wingos' tiger is modeled after one used to promote a Columbia, South Carolina, gas station; the relocation of Colleton is inspired by the movement of Ellington, South Carolina, for a nuclear facility; and Tolitha's testing of coffins is based on Conroy's experience with his own beloved grandmother, Stanny.[14]

As had been true of his earlier books, *The Prince of Tides* created ripples within the Conroy family.[15] Carol Conroy, upon whom Savannah was closely modeled, withdrew her support for the novel, refusing to allow Conroy to use her poetry in *The Prince of Tides* as had been planned.[16] Shortly thereafter she cut off all communication with him. Their schism seems improbable given the shared sensibility of their fictional doppelgängers, but even this relationship is erased in Conroy's later fiction: the protagonists of *Beach Music* and *South of Broad,* his next two novels, have only brothers. Carol haunts Conroy's most recent memoir, *The Death of Santini,* however, and while he always speaks of her poetry in the most admiring of terms, he is constantly shifting in his understanding of her in the book, sometimes depicting her outrageous—and often humorless—acts utterly without sympathy and at times mourning the loss of the of their relationship as "best of friends."

Indeed the publication of *The Prince of Tides* was followed by a series of ruptures in the Conroy family that were only slightly less dramatic than the collective anger that had followed *The Great Santini.* While Peggy Conroy knew that she would have a role in *The Prince of Tides,* she did not live to see the novel's publication, and Conroy has said, perhaps with some relief, "I can't make a guess about how much I think my mother would've hated that book."[17] Don Conroy, on the other hand, was free with his contempt. While he displayed none of the explosiveness that he had upon discovering his portrait in Bull Meecham, in the wake of the release of *The Prince of Tides,* he adopted an attitude of studied bemusement that suggested that Conroy's work was an act of misplaced spite.[18] His continued denial of the abuse he had committed against his family threatened the tentative truce that he and Pat had formed and created factions within the siblings.[19] The death of Conroy's mother, then, was quickly followed by the loss of Carol and a larger sense of unrest within the family. By 1991 Conroy found himself on the precipice of another major depression, completing the damaging cycle that had established itself with his earlier literary forays into his own history.

CHAPTER 6

Beach Music

The Prince of Tides was completed during a period of significant change for Conroy; his next novel, *Beach Music* (1995), published almost nine years later, was written during a period of great physical and emotional upheaval. After leaving Rome he settled in Atlanta, but he soured on the city after becoming embroiled the cultural melee surrounding the firing of *Atlanta Journal and Constitution* editor Bill Kovach and moved to San Francisco in 1989 at his wife Lenore's urging.[1] California was not the refuge that Conroy had imagined, however; by his account, Lenore quickly "got caught up in the whirlpool of high society," and Conroy found his writing time regularly interrupted by social obligations.[2] Balance from the "baronial" qualities of life in San Francisco was provided by an old Beaufort friend, Tim Belk, who was living in the city and had been diagnosed with AIDS.[3] Belk had played an important role in encouraging Conroy's intellectual development during his early years in Beaufort, and the move to San Francisco had appealed to him in part because he saw an opportunity to help his friend. Through Belk he soon learned about the despair and suffering the AIDS epidemic had wrought within San Francisco's gay community, and Conroy felt himself called to reach out to those who had no other advocate; during his time in San Francisco, "Tim and I made it our mission to hunt out southern boys abandoned by their families, disgusted by their homosexuality, and left to die alone."[4] While Conroy would fictionalize this experience more directly in *South of Broad,* his contact with men suffering from loneliness, shame, and fear—as well as the immediate physical consequences of AIDS—certainly informed his work on *Beach Music.*

The anguish Conroy encountered in his work with Belk was also echoed in his domestic life: his troubled marriage to Lenore was nearing its end, and their separation would bring about a lasting estrangement from his daughter

Susannah; his stepdaughter, Emily, who was living with the Conroys in San Francisco, made a series of suicide attempts; and in his final year in California, Conroy was hit by a car and laid up for months with excruciating back pain. These stresses were aggravated by the extraordinary pressure he felt to finish *Beach Music*, now several years overdue. Conroy was aware of Doubleday's significant investment in the book, and in fact he was experiencing his own financial strains.[5] In addition Conroy was also understandably anxious about the expectations that were being placed on his work: when asked by an interviewer how he approached writing after the enormous success of *The Prince of Tides*, Conroy replied, "Tremblingly. It was scary for a while, and it remains somewhat scary."[6] Given these overlapping emotional, physical, economic, and artistic pressures, it is not surprising that Conroy suffered another nervous breakdown in 1993, and he left San Francisco—and his marriage—to seek treatment once again from the therapist who had helped him work through previous depressions, Dr. Marion O'Neill, in South Carolina. He recalls the period as one of the most difficult of his life, and he has explained that even as he was making progress on *Beach Music*, "I could not shake the obsessional urge to end my life. I found myself shopping for pistols in pawn shops, studying the veins of wrist and throat, and learning how to get to the roof of the DeSoto Hilton in Savannah."[7]

While he was able to emerge from "the black voyage of spirit," Conroy's sense of himself was rocked again in August 1994 when his brother Tom, a paranoid schizophrenic, killed himself by jumping off a building.[8] Conroy had modeled a character in *Beach Music* after Tom, John Hardin McCall, and at the time of Tom's death, he had already written a scene in the novel in which John Hardin commits suicide. Even given the close relationship between life and fiction that marks almost all of Conroy's work, Tom's death was a startling manifestation of the uncanny, and the scene took on a newly painful resonance. Consequently Conroy rewrote John Hardin's narrative so that he never made an attempt on his life, a literary resurrection that functioned as the emotional inverse of killing off Bull Meecham in *The Great Santini*. Yet despite this choice the novel hardly can be said to sidestep grief or to ignore the consequences of madness and violence; indeed *Beach Music* is Conroy's darkest—and most ambitious—work to date.

The novel's principal narrative is centered on Jack McCall, a food writer who moves with his young daughter to Rome after the suicide of his wife, Shyla. Early in the novel, however, he is called back to South Carolina when his mother, Lucy—a thinly veiled Peggy Conroy—is diagnosed with advanced leukemia, and once there Jack must confront not only the realities of his own past but the often traumatic histories of his family members and of a group of friends who have been close since childhood. The domestic focus of *The Prince of Tides* and *The Great Santini* is still evident in *Beach Music,* but in this novel Conroy looks beyond the politics of a single family to consider the ways that personal and cultural histories shape one another as they run parallel to one another and, as often, collide. *Beach Music* displays a historical reach that is new to Conroy's work, weaving together stories of psychological and physical suffering that are rooted not only in the contemporary South but in the Ukraine during the Russian Revolution and Poland during the Holocaust.[9] In engaging such disparate narratives, *Beach Music* expands upon questions of identity that inform his earlier work and remaps them in a series of varied geographical and historical contexts. The result is an unexpected cultural bricolage that considers the ways in which personal and collective traumas may be understood and rendered meaningful.

The new direction of Conroy's work stymied many critics. If *The Prince of Tides* generated wide public admiration, *Beach Music* was a considerably more polarizing book: its heft—the paperback comes in at more than 750 pages—and its scope led some reviewers to claim that Conroy's already baroque style had become so exaggerated that it obfuscated the central narrative.[10] Moreover reviewers suggested that in attempting to tell so many stories, each suffused with intense drama, Conroy had sacrificed the narrative intimacy that had defined his earlier, more tightly focused work.[11] Some of these criticisms seem fair, and in many ways *Beach Music* is indeed more notable for its most effective set pieces than for its identity as a coherent whole. Yet in gathering a diverse group of vignettes, often narrated by characters of different ages and experiences than those who populate his previous works, Conroy underscores the metanarrative qualities of the novel as well: always insistent on his identity as a storyteller, Conroy uses *Beach Music* not only as a canvas for new stories but as a way of exploring the power of narrative itself.

This instinct is revealed early in the novel when Jack references his practice of telling his daughter, Leah, stories as a way of allowing her to access a history from which she is removed. Because Shyla died when Leah was just two and Jack moved with her to Rome shortly afterward, Leah has no real memories of family beyond her father, and thus the stories that he shares with her becomes crucial in her self-imagining. Jack observes that Leah's favorite story is of the night he and Shyla fell in love, a narrative that bathes her parents' relationship in the light of romance and forecasts Leah's own entry into the family narrative. The tale has adopted "a fixed, by-the-numbers quality as rote as a catechist's response" (9), a characterization that underscores the ways in which stories have become a form of faith to both Leah and Jack, offering the comfort of tradition and the reassurance of the existence of a larger truth. Yet Leah's love of Jack's

"Chippie" stories is equally revealing. Jack has created a series of myths loosely based on real events in his history in which his childhood dog is recast as "the Great Dog Chippie," a canine superhero who saves the otherwise helpless protagonist. Those who had known Chippie raise their eyebrows when they hear of the dog's elevated status—Jack's mother, Lucy, observes, "She was a mutt, for God's sake" (296)—but Leah is untroubled by such skepticism, because she recognizes and accepts Chippie as an invention. Indeed Leah acknowledges that she "only like[s] Great Dog Chippie stories when [she's] feeling sad" (276) and, presumably, is in need of a powerful fictional surrogate. The stories Jack tells Leah exist primarily in two competing modes then: the stories about her family and the South are meant to give Leah a clearer sense of her own identity, while the stories about Chippie are designed to relieve her from its burdens.

This essential contradiction becomes important in understanding the complex function of stories within the novel. Jack is hobbled by the same inability to express emotion that Conroy ascribes to southern men throughout his work, and thus he often tells Leah a story when a subject is too tender to address openly. (And, showing a wisdom beyond her years, Leah frequently requests a story when she feels Jack cannot speak to her more directly, a dynamic that is illustrated in their visit to Shyla's grave.) Yet while stories are seen as a crucial conduit of expression, their role becomes complicated when Jack talks to Leah about the nature of stories themselves. When Leah first meets Lucy, she asks if her grandmother is a good storyteller, and with a wryness meant more for himself than Leah, Jack responds, "She was the best. No one could lie like my mother" (275). When Leah asks about his equation of stories and lies, though, he backpedals, deciding that "[a] story is never a lie. A story gives only pleasure. A lie gives mostly pain" (276). Jack's conclusion seems to be a condemnation of his mother rather than a true assessment of the function of stories, however, and he later revises this judgment, telling Leah, "Stories don't have to be true. They just have to help" (301). His contradictory observations here—as well as the competing motivations for the stories that he tells Leah—play an important role throughout the novel, and as characters seek salvation by either sharing or hearing stories that are central to their histories, the divisions between truth and lies, fact and myth, and pleasure and pain become obscured.

This is evinced most clearly in the novel's inclusion of four narratives that exist as individual set pieces: Max Russoff's story of his violent coming-of-age in the Ukraine, Ruth Fox's account of her escape from the Nazis, George Fox's recollection of living under Nazi rule in Poland, and Lucy McCall's confessions about her upbringing in the Deep South. Collectively these stories shape the larger narrative of *Beach Music,* grounding its contemporary plot in a traumatic history. Yet the revelations inherent in each individual story are also

testaments to the relative dangers of narrative; with the exception of Max, each
storyteller is deeply anxious about the ways their disclosures—and, equally,
their elisions and occultations—may affect their listeners.

Max's tale is the first to be featured in the novel, and it is as disturbing as the
ones that follow it. His story is about a pogrom that takes place when he was a
young man living in the Ukraine, an unimaginably violent tale that reaches its
climax when Max witnesses two Cossacks raping the young woman he loves.
Driven to action, he kills them with a meat cleaver, later butchering the men's
horses to hide his crime. The Jewish community is unable to sort through its
own responses to Max's actions, and ultimately he is sent to America in an
act of ostracism. The details of his experience may be shocking to Conroy's
readers, but interestingly the story itself is rendered benign to Max's listeners
through its telling. Indeed his history has become a celebrated myth in Waterford, South Carolina, the community that embraced Max as "the Great Jew"
upon his immigration: Jack says he has heard the story "a dozen times as a boy
growing up in Waterford" (214) and, in turn, has laid claim to it himself, telling
it to "everyone I meet in Italy" (213). Early in the novel, then, Max's story functions as a testament to the liberation that results when one claims one's history
even as it unfolds. In Max's case the story he tells frees him from shame and, as
significantly, empowers his listeners.

Max is alone in this relationship to his history, however, and *Beach Music* is
more concerned with the ways that a narrative can warp both its narrator and
its audience. Jack's mother-in-law, Ruth Fox, for example, believes that it is the
story she has shared about her experience with "the lady of the coins" that triggered her daughter Shyla's hallucinations, depression, and, ultimately, suicide.
The story recalls Ruth's orphaning at the hands of the Nazis, and at its center
it recounts the perceived sympathy Ruth senses in a statue of the Virgin Mary;
she uses the sculpture as a hiding place for coins her mother has given her to
help in her safe passage, and Ruth finds herself praying to Mary "as Jewish girl
to Jewish girl" (502). Not long after Ruth tells Shyla the story, Shyla experiences
hallucinations in which she is visited by Mary, and shortly thereafter she is institutionalized. "If I had not told Shyla this story," Ruth tells Jack, "maybe my
daughter would be with us now" (507). In telling a story so unconventional in
its nature and oppressive in its details, Ruth suggests, she has not merely opened
her history to Shyla but invited her to share it, a burden that ultimately proves
to be fatal.

Conversely Ruth's husband, George Fox, believes that it is the story he did
not tell Shyla that drove her to despair. He explains to Jack that he has never
shared his experiences during the Holocaust because he thinks that "anyone
who heard [the whole story] would never be able to sleep again or have any

peace." After Shyla's death, however, George determines that "a story untold could be the one that kills you" (509). The story is, indeed, almost unbearable: George finds himself complicit in the Nazis' most unthinkable atrocities when he is appointed a member of the Judenrat, a group who must choose the members of their community who will be killed and, later, when he serves as a laborer in the gas chambers at Auschwitz. He is a survivor of the Holocaust only in a physical sense; plagued by memories and grief, George never fully inhabits his life after he is liberated, and he tells Jack that after the Holocaust, "I can only love phantoms" (635). The history that George does not share is not rendered invisible but becomes a defining lacuna in Shyla's life, and her adulthood is defined by an attempt to rewrite her father's history: Shyla becomes a peace activist during the Vietnam War so that she can stand up for those she sees as victimized and powerless, and when she and Jack have their own daughter, she showers Leah with love. Ultimately, however, Shyla is driven to connect with her family's spectral history by reenacting it. In the midst of one of her depressions, she has the number her father was assigned at Auschwitz tattooed on her own arm and jumps off a bridge in an act of imagined communion with the Jews who perished there.

The Foxes' conflicting beliefs that they have shared too much or too little with their daughter can never be resolved. In telling their stories to Jack, however, they do recognize a value in the act of storytelling. Both Ruth and George offer their stories as acts of reparation for the custody battle for Leah that they had instigated after Shyla's death, an ugly fight in which they told a series of painful lies in a desperate attempt to sway the judge. By telling the truth now, Ruth and Gorge use narrative to recuperative ends, and even as Ruth begins her story, Jack understands that "by telling me what happened to her . . . Ruth was handing over to me a gift of extraordinary value. By informing me of her history, she was demonstrating her own need to close the door on our embattled past." This "gift" has a secondary value as well: Jack notes that "Ruth was providing me with some key to the mystery of Shyla's death" (492). In fact in sharing their Holocaust narratives with Jack, the Foxes allow themselves to consider Shyla's death more fully as well. Ruth confesses to Jack that "if I had explained to you the meaning of 'the lady of the coins' [earlier] . . . then I could not have blamed you for Shyla's death. . . . I blamed you so that I would not plunge into despair" (239). To deny history may temporarily stave off the agony of its truths, but as Ruth suggests here, suppressed histories condemn their subjects to a crippling stasis. To tell a personal truth, she suggests, is to allow for the unfolding of a collective history.

Lucy's decision to share her story is perhaps the most dramatic illustration of this notion in the novel. Like most of the mothers who inhabit Conroy's

work, Lucy is an act of furious self-creation, and she has inspired a deep ambivalence in her sons, who as adults have grown weary of her steady manipula-
tion of them. When Jack believes that Lucy is tracking him down in Rome, for
instance, he refers to her as "my goddamn untrustworthy, back-stabbing, pain-
in-the ass mother" (32), and when he receives a telegram that states that she is
dying of leukemia, he laughs, believing that she is "not even sick. . . . She's just
after something. Something big. Lucy's a great strategist" (103). Yet Jack often
softens when he thinks of his mother, and he recognizes that he has "[grown]
up much too close to her, much too in love with her, dazzled by . . . her famous
beauty" (164). Like Lila Wingo in *The Prince of Tides,* Lucy is unknowable—
Jack identifies her as "mysterious, unplaceable, [and] night-shaped" (573)—
and thus, like Lila, she is equally dangerous in each of her myriad of facades.

When Jack realizes that his mother is indeed dying, he finds some of his
uncertainties about her are temporarily quashed, but their relationship undergoes a more authentic shift when she decides to tell him about her childhood.
Up until that point, Lucy had offered a flimsy narrative of her childhood, one,
we later learn, that she has adapted from a story she heard while working in
a strip club. Her mother-in-law, Ginny Penn, recognizes Lucy's forged heritage
immediately, but because she meets Lucy after she has married her son, she is
compelled to accept the narrative or to risk ridicule herself, an important lesson
for Lucy about the ways that fictions can be transformed into truths. Indeed
throughout her adulthood Lucy continues to occupy others' histories with increasing confidence; for example in an unlikely turn of events, she inherits one
of Waterford's most storied houses and finds that the sense of history it conveys
is "transfigur[ing]" in its conferral of authority (260). Lucy's performance as a
southern belle takes a more literal turn when she dons a "Southern plantation
dress" each year for Waterford's house tour (262). She becomes the highlight
of the tour after perfecting an impassioned version of the story of Elizabeth
Cotesworth, a young woman who had once lived in the house and who had so
charmed William Sherman that he had refused to burn Charleston as a gift to
her. Dressed in clothes that resemble Elizabeth's and narrating her life story,
Lucy happily embraces her role as Elizabeth's self-appointed surrogate, and
when she names one of her sons Tecumseh after Sherman's middle name, she
suggests the legitimacy of her inheritance.

Ultimately, however, the bedrock of Lucy's identity is entirely fabricated, and
the story she finally shares with Jack has little in common with the antebellum
romance in which Elizabeth Cotesworth stars and instead functions as an almost
perfect example of the southern gothic.[12] In it Lucy's mother kills her abusive
husband in front of Lucy and later hangs herself in the same room where Lucy
and her brother, Jude, are sleeping. The horrors of their experiences continue

after they are abandoned: Lucy is repeatedly raped by the minister who runs the orphanage where she and Jude are placed, and Jude, who is just eight years old, kills him in an act of careful premeditation one night. While Jude ultimately finds his place—and consequently a lasting faith—in a Catholic orphanage in Charleston, Lucy finds herself on the streets at age thirteen, and her first sense of stability comes with her marriage to Johnson Hagood McCall. Here she can adopt the script of a lawyer's wife and young mother until she inhabits the roles with genuine confidence. Yet Johnson Hagood's alcoholism and abusiveness are reminders of the ways in which her past is not erased but rather exists as a still-visible layer in a hastily composed palimpsest, and Lucy is never able to abandon the vigilance that had been required of her childhood. Throughout her marriage —and indeed after her divorce from Johnson Hagood and her marriage to Dr. Pitts—Lucy is engaged in a series of endless performances that simultaneously comfort and unsettle her five sons in ways they are incapable of fully identifying or understanding.

Like the stories Max Russoff and the Foxes tell, Lucy's history is a self-contained narrative within the novel, and Jack never overtly reflects upon Lucy's history in his own narration.[13] Yet despite its relative brevity and its discreteness, Lucy's story has an enormous impact within the novel, demonstrating that the monstrous can be rendered sympathetic through narrative. After Jack knows Lucy's story, the caustic edge that marks his tone in his earliest references to his mother diminishes significantly. Because he has a new context for considering Lucy and because he now understands that, as her eldest son, he and Lucy "grew up together" (719), he is able not only to forgive his mother but also to appreciate her. By contrast, for example, Johnson Hagood remains inscrutable throughout the novel; while we are given glimpses of him as a bright young lawyer throughout the narrative, we are never exposed to his history in a meaningful way. As a result we see him primarily as an embodiment of alcoholic malice, and his identity as a heartless cipher speaks to the narrative fate that Lucy might have shared.

The impact of Lucy's story can also be felt in the fact that Jack and Lucy's reconciliation is cemented when Jack reads her a series of children's books in her final days. Most immediately this act represents the full reversal of the roles of parent and child, but it also speaks to the fact that both of them recognize the power of narrative to provide peace: Lucy has provided Jack with an important story that allows him to think about his childhood in new ways, and now he is providing her with the stories that "she had missed" in her own deprived childhood (748).

Lucy's narrative also resonates in the novel in that it provides Jack with insight into himself. Most obviously her story helps to explain why the McCalls are Catholic, which Jack has identified in a moment of exasperation as "a ridiculous, brain-dead, dimwitted, sexually perverse, odd-duck, know-nothing, silly-assed church" (411). Throughout the novel he struggles with his Catholicism, which, as it has for Conroy's earlier protagonists, isolated him in the Protestant South, and it has also taunted him with a vision of faith that remains out of his grasp: Jack is often overcome by the beauty of Italian churches and the sublimity of the language of the Catholic service, but when he attends church he notes that "I felt the Mass going through me, but not touching me" (290). While, unlike Jack, Lucy is a "good" Catholic, her history suggests that she too may be "untouched." In her brother, Jude, however, she has witnessed the power of faith to transform: his destiny is altered when he becomes a Trappist monk and thus finds a literal and spiritual home through his faith. Lucy may have succeeded in her quest for validation, but Jude has found true redemption, and thus Lucy has raised her sons as Catholics in part because of Jude's testament to the potential power of faith.

These themes—history, violence, faith, and reconciliation—are repeated more broadly in the novel's contemporary plot line, in which Jack attempts to make sense of his own experience by unearthing the story of his tight-knit group of six friends. Certainly Jack is an unlikely historian at best: he asserts that "the thing I love about the past most is not thinking about it" (55), and he has moved to Rome not only because of his love for the city but also because it allows him to escape into a history and culture that is not his own. As a travel and food writer, he is a perpetual tourist, and he takes comfort in the fact that his job "keeps me at arm's length from the subjects that are too close to me" (77). Moreover Italy's geographical distance from South Carolina provides a vital physical reinforcement of its emotional buffer. The novel's title, *Beach Music,* references the Carolina shag music that serves as the background for Jack and Shyla's romance, but Lucy redefines the term when she shares her theory for why her beloved loggerhead turtles instinctively crawl toward the sea shortly after they have hatched from their eggs: "I think they listen to the waves. I think they just love beach music" (578). In moving to Italy, Jack has sought to place himself outside the call of home; like Lucy—and more broadly the Foxes—he actively distances himself from his history as a way of denying its painfulness.

Jack is finally compelled to delve into his own history, though, when he is approached by his friend Mike Hess, now a Hollywood producer, who commissions Jack and another friend, Ledare Ansley, to coauthor a miniseries based on their coterie's experiences. Mike reveals that the project is meaningful to him because he feels divorced from his history and cannot connect with his early idealism; the series Ledare and Jack will create, he suggests, will give a sense of coherence to their individual and shared experiences. While Jack does not acknowledge it—he ostensibly takes the job for the money—he may crave this sense of historical connection, too. His return home has left him feeling dislocated, and while he has taken up his assigned role among his brothers, this return to the fold has provided him with little insight or connection. As he notes early in the novel, his relationship with his brothers is largely "inscrutable and promissory" (116), and while there are moments of true fraternal communion in the novel, they are fleeting. Indeed the McCall brothers' relationships with one another are defined primarily by a shared, wincing humor, and while the brothers understand one another, none seems stable enough to offer meaningful support to the others, save the care they offer their youngest brother, John Hardin, whose schizophrenia functions as an exaggerated expression of their collective disorientation.

Jack's friends, then, have become a crucial surrogate family, and at its heart is Jack's friendship with Jordan Elliott. If Jack is, in many ways, the quintessential Conroy protagonist, Jordan is his perfect complement: in *Beach Music* it is Jordan who is the military brat caught between his father's eternal disappointment and his mother's soft love, a dilemma that is familiar to Conroy's readers. Unlike Ben Meecham or Will McLean, however, Jordan possesses an unimaginable confidence. While Ben and Will are driven by a need to conform, Jordan continually resists the expectations of Waterford, often with remarkable effect: he immediately bests the school bully upon arriving in town, he establishes himself as the best athlete at the high school, and he introduces his new friends to elements of West Coast cool. Moreover in his skepticism he seems more perceptive than his friends, appreciating Shyla's quiet beauty, for example, or thinking through the problems of survival in an extended episode when the boys are set adrift at sea after Capers Middleton, the most arrogant and entitled member of the group, tries to catch a giant manta ray.

Throughout the novel, then, Jordan exists as a curious hybrid, a figure who is at once recognizable and at the same time utterly exotic, and his friends' undeniable fascination with him is echoed in his clear authority within the narrative. Although he is a relative newcomer to the group, he comes to function as their collective conscience, an embodiment of their best selves. When the group graduates from high school, Jack, Mike, Capers, Ledare, and Shyla all head to the University of South Carolina, where they occupy comfortable roles: Jack finds pleasure as an English major, Capers and Ledare embrace Greek life, Mike becomes a serious film student and photographer, and Shyla devotes herself to her studies. Jordan, however, is sent to the Citadel in an act that is designed to remold him in his father's image. The situation is untenable, and Jordan orchestrates a daring plan to have himself thrown out of school for becoming involved in a prank against Furman University, the Citadel's rival, finding a solution that simultaneously frees him to join his friends and leaves his honor intact.

The sort of blithe acceptance of southern identity that marks Jack's childhood friends' early college experience, along with the elegant balancing of independence and obligation that Jordan demonstrates at the Citadel, ends when they are confronted with the realities of the Vietnam War. Until this point there had been a largely predictable dynamic within the group, disturbed only occasionally by the different romantic configurations that emerged within their ranks over the years. The war puts an end to the idyllically ahistorical quality of their friendships, however, and the story that emerges is deeply entangled with the disorienting politics of the time. We learn that Capers has pretended to be a part of the antiwar movement at the university but in fact is working for the South Carolina Law Enforcement Division. After leading Jack, Jordan, and Shyla (then his girlfriend) to a Selective Service Office where they destroy draft files, Capers then testifies against them.[14] Capers's claim that their patriotic infidelity trumps his own personal betrayals leaves the group ideologically fractured and emotionally shattered.

The individual cost of Capers's betrayal is greatest for Jordan. Like his friends Jordan is arrested after the break-in, but while Jack and Shyla are tried and given a suspended sentence, Jordan's father, Gen. Rembert Elliott, has Jordan institutionalized. He is locked up in the South Carolina State Hospital for almost a year, the same institution to which Shyla and John Hardin are sent after their hallucinatory breaks with reality, and while he is there he is given a series of shock treatments and antipsychotic medications. Jordan's experience is a powerful testament to the ease with which personal and political "madness" can be conflated and, as significant, to the absolute nature of patriarchal power. Indeed while General Elliott has always been a menacing and violent figure, after Jordan's arrest it becomes almost impossible to distinguish between the patriarchy and the pater; just as the country is refusing to listen to the voice of youth dissent, Elliott refuses to provide support for his son. In his narrative Jack includes a tableau in which Elliott strikes Jordan in public—and in front of photographers—in a scene that is laden with symbolism. Considering a photo of the event, he notes that in his "iconic fury" Elliott "represented America to adults, but to us he stood for everything that was tyrannical and immovable and dissembling in the American spirit turned leprous by Vietnam" (683–84). For Jack the slap is the condemnation of a generation of Americans who cannot understand his stance toward war; for Jordan, however, it also represents the very literal contempt of his father.

After he is released from the hospital, Jordan tries to develop a strategy that will both punish his father and free himself from their drama, one that exists in the model of his successful plan to extract himself from the Citadel. This time, however, Jordan is not so lucky. He decides to blow up a plane on his father's base as an act of protest and then to fake his own suicide. The plan goes awry, though, because two young lovers using the plane for a tryst are killed in the explosion. What is meant to be a victimless crime has suddenly become an act of murder, and Jordan's attempt to distance himself from both his father's unyielding forcefulness and the senseless violence of Vietnam actually yokes him to them. Already cast into exile by his presumed death, Jordan escapes to Canada and later travels to Europe, where he becomes a Trappist monk. Here his story dovetails with the historical narratives that have been relayed earlier in the novel: like Jude, he finds both faith and a calling through violence. He explains that "I was born to be a priest, but I had to kill two innocent people to find that out" (709). And like the Foxes and Lucy, Jordan finds himself haunted by his untold story. While a great deal of the contemporary plot thread is concerned with Mike's desire to confirm that Jordan is alive and compel him to tell his story, in fact Jordan decides on his own that he wants to explain his choices and share his experiences.

This conversation takes an unconventional form when Mike arranges a mock trial for Jordan, one that is attended by Jordan's parents and friends and that is presided over by a surprisingly sober and sharp Johnson Hagood Mc-Call. The trial is an artificial plot contrivance in some ways, but its theatricality also seems fitting given the fact that it is Mike's handiwork. Conditioned by years in Hollywood, he can only think in terms of sensational plot twists and melodramatic emotions, and he has gone to great lengths to stage a confrontation that he believes will be rewarding to an audience. Jordan's participation, though, is the most interesting component of the trial. It is later revealed that he has agreed to turn himself in to the authorities even before he appears as a defendant in Mike's trial, and so he participates primarily as a way of sharing his history with his family and friends. In accepting his role in the trial, then, he asks for their judgment as a means of allowing them to respond to his story rather than to decide his fate. Jordan's trial invites a more formal referendum than Max's, the Foxes', or Lucy's stories, but it serves the same role in that it allows Jordan to be free of his shame and invites his listeners to understand him—and themselves—more fully.

As *Beach Music* concludes, Jordan is beginning a five-year term for manslaughter, a sentence that acknowledges his good work as a priest in Italy and, in fact, will allow him to continue his work in prison, which he equates to another form of monastic cell. Moreover in a parallel to Jack and Lucy's reconciliation, Jordan and Rembert Elliott have formed a once-inconceivable bond, and Rembert, who alone had voted that Jordan must turn himself in, supports

his son throughout his trial and moves to be closer to the prison in which he is
incarcerated. The novel's remaining loose ends are tied together as well: Lucy
dies with her family gathered around her, and in a scene suggestive of her redemption, shortly after her death Jack and Leah revive one of the sea turtles
she had worked so hard to protect, walking it out into the ocean in a scene that
recalls both baptism and resurrection. Jack's loneliness comes to an end, too;
in working with Ledare to write the history of their group of friends, the two
are able to envision a future together, and at the novel's close they are married
in Italy, surrounded by almost all of their friends from Waterford.

This otherwise tidy conclusion is troubled only when Jack shares Shyla's suicide letter with Ledare shortly before they are married. In it Shyla makes an eternal claim to Jack, writing that after her death he should "marry a nice woman . . .
but not one so nice that you won't want to get back to me in our house beneath
the sea" (759). She is referring to her first dance with Jack, one that took place
years before they began to date seriously and was remarkable not only in the
ways that it foreshadowed the romantic nature of their relationship, but also
its perilousness: they danced together in a condemned beach house just as it
gave in to the power of erosion. The dance is, of course, charged with symbolism. In their youthfulness Shyla and Jack are thrilled by their own risk-taking
and electrified by the romance of the ocean's power. They are less aware of the
ways in which the destruction of the house symbolizes their own vulnerability.
Ultimately, their dance suggests, no place is safe, even the intimate spaces of
home, and Shyla's death by drowning imbues the idea of an underwater house
with a new sadness. Ledare's response to the note demonstrates the ways in
which the resolutions of the various threads of the novel have shaped Jack's
life, however. She quite reasonably identifies the note as "intimidating" but then
tells Jack, "Let's love each other as well as we can. But Shyla can have the last
dance. She earned it" (759). Ledare indicates here that the past and the future
can comfortably coexist and that history does not have to be denied or dwelled
upon, but can simply inform the present. In this way the darkest of Conroy's
novels concludes with an unexpected sunniness, and *Beach Music,* a novel written during a period of personal despair for Conroy, suggests that narrative has
the power of salvation.

CHAPTER 7

My Losing Season

Beach Music's epic scope is balanced by the much narrower focus of Conroy's next work, *My Losing Season* (2002), a memoir that considers his experiences as a basketball player during his senior year at the Citadel. Sports play a crucial role in the development of almost all of Conroy's fictional protagonists—indeed, one reviewer defines the quintessential Conroy hero as a "sensitive southern jock"[1]—but athletic competition is made central in *My Losing Season,* which relives each of the games the Citadel Bulldogs played during the 1966–67 season. The book represents an unexpected departure in some ways: in returning to memoir, Conroy was temporarily abandoning the genre in which he had achieved his greatest successes, and as Nan Talese cautioned, he risked losing his female readership by writing a book that was explicitly about college basketball.[2] Such fears were quickly dispelled, though. While it has not equaled the sales of his novels, *My Losing Season* is a success by most other measures: it was widely celebrated by reviewers—"Conroy's Literary Slam-Dunk" is a typical headline—and it has found an enthusiastic audience in women as well as men: Conroy has remarked that "I've had whole girls' basketball teams come to book signings."[3]

While *My Losing Season* is undeniably a sports memoir, it is an unconventional example of the genre. Most obviously, unlike books that recall record-breaking accomplishments, Conroy's memoir chronicles a season defined primarily by defeat: the Citadel's record that year was eight wins and seventeen losses. As a college player—and, indeed, as a middle-aged memoirist—Conroy is devastated by each loss and, more specifically, by his own inability to play to the level of his expectations at times. As a result *My Losing Season* testifies to "the intense and permanent scar-power of sport at all levels," as Grainger David wrote in his review of the book. David sees the memoir as speaking to ex-jocks who are now "lawyers, accountants, salesmen, [and] sportswriters," and certainly *My Losing Season* has a specific appeal to those who have walked in—and reluctantly left behind—Conroy's Converse All Stars.[4] But the memoir has a wider reach in that Conroy's account of his final season of college basketball offers him a way of thinking about his life more broadly, and reviewer Robert W. Creamer makes the fairly bold claim that "*My Losing Season* is Conroy's *apologia pro vita sua* [defense of his life]."[5] Ultimately, then, Conroy's depictions of the camaraderie, competition, and, inevitably, the crushing defeats of his basketball career not only are captivating in themselves but also function as an inventive lens through which to reconsider many of the themes that have defined his fictional oeuvre and, as significant, to consider the ways his life and fiction have impacted one another.

For Conroy basketball is a lifelong passion, and at its most basic level, *My Losing Season* is a testament to the joy inherent in the instinctive expression of physical ambition. Conroy traces his love of the sport to his childhood, and he identifies himself as a "rawboned kid who fell in love with the smell and shape of a basketball, who longed for its smooth skin on the nerve endings of my fingers and hands, who lived for the sound of its unmistakable heartbeat, its staccato rhythms, as I bounced it along the pavement throughout the ten thousand days of my boyhood" (2). This love of the game proved transformative in Conroy's life. As a military brat whose family's regular moves kept him from establishing a stable group of friends, basketball offered a crucial social shortcut; as Conroy notes, "Games allowed me to introduce myself to people who had never heard me speak out loud, to earn their praise without uttering a single word" (1). Indeed he was voted president of his high school senior class after having lived in Beaufort, South Carolina, for little more than a year, a fact he attributes in large part to his stature on the basketball team. As important, however, as a child basketball offered Conroy an escape from the abusive Don Conroy. Not only were basketball courts a safe haven, but they also presented a "legitimate physical outlet for all the violence and rage and sadness" he could not express elsewhere (6). As he grew older, Conroy saw basketball as a means to a more permanent escape: a scholarship was his best shot of going to college and thus of achieving the autonomy and stability he was denied by Don. In an ironic twist, however, his only real offer came from the Citadel, and he was not given an athletic scholarship for his first year but was offered a spot as a walk-on player. As a result Conroy found himself at an institution that replicated his father's worldview and at the mercy of a coaching staff who, like Don, withheld their sanction.

Thus while *My Losing Season* is devoted primarily to telling the story of Conroy and his teammates during their ill-fated year, it is not surprising that

Don repeatedly appears in the book and, even when he is not present, that Don and Pat's relationship shades Conroy's understanding of himself as a player. He notes that sports have always functioned as an important point of connection with his father, and at times it is their *only* connection: he notes succinctly, "If not for sports, I do not think my father ever would have talked to me" (6). Basketball is the primary language he shares with his father, a former college hall-of-fame player, and it also becomes a way of understanding, and even emulating, Don; early in the memoir, Conroy acknowledges that "basketball allowed me to revere my father without him knowing what I was up to. I took up basketball as a form of homage and mimicry" (47). As Conroy's readers might expect, however, Don does not embrace his role as a mentor; Conroy notes that while he "could've taught me everything about basketball I'd need to know . . . instead, he taught me nothing. . . . A beautiful shooter, a fierce rebounder, and a legendary defender, my father chose not to pass these ineffable skills on to any of his five sons. We grew up overshadowed by his legend and that legend did not lift a finger to help us toward any patch of light our own small achievements might have granted us" (48).

The suggestion that Don hoards his knowledge as a way of ensuring his dominance over his sons is reinforced in his refusal to support Conroy's basketball career in any manner. He comes to only two games during Conroy's senior year at the Citadel and adopts a practice of showing no emotion when Conroy is playing well. Out of the stands, Don is more vocal in his discouragement. Before Conroy's senior year in high school, for example, he cruelly predicts that "you [will] score less than ten [points] a game this year. . . . I bet not a single college scout comes to watch you play" (79), and he continues to make such dire forecasts throughout Conroy's college career, suggesting, for example, that as a senior he will be replaced as point guard by Tee Hooper, a younger, taller, and perhaps more gifted player. Hooper is not Conroy's real competition in Don's mind, though; instead it is Don's legacy that is being threatened, and he takes pleasure in telling Conroy, "You couldn't hold my jock as a ballplayer" (242).

To readers acquainted with Bull Meecham, Don's casual sadism is more familiar than it is shocking; what is surprising, however, is that Conroy finds himself playing for a college coach who seems to be Don's spiritual twin. Like Don, Citadel coach Mel Thompson refuses to praise his players in any way—Conroy notes that Thompson tells him "Good game" only once (84), and the compliment comes during the period in which he is being recruited to the team—and instead he demeans his players as a way of motivating them. This alone may not be terribly remarkable in the world of college basketball, but Thompson seems to have taken all his moves from Santini's playbook. Like Don, who refuses to teach his sons the secrets of his game, Thompson "was inarticulate when it came to explaining how a defense was supposed to work. He screamed a lot, but there was little teaching going on" (29). And just as Don insists upon undermining Conroy's sense of self by predicting his failures, Thompson inexplicably—and, it turns out, erroneously—sells Conroy short at the beginning of his senior season, telling a local reporter that he is good for "one or two points a game" (31). (Conroy in fact averages twelve points a game and scores a remarkable twenty-five points in his best game.)

More globally, in seeking to make his players "tougher," Thompson takes an approach that echoes the unrelenting brutality of the fathers who populate Conroy's earlier work. Conroy reports, for example, that Thompson "would search for the soft spots and breaking points of his newest players, then would go to work on them with a cruel finesse" (25). While this coaching strategy is designed to make his players "more resilient when the games came down to the wire" (25), it is also remarkably similar to Johnson Hagood McCall's tactic of "kid-fucking," which he outlines for Jack in Beach Music: "You find out where [your kids] are weakest. You work away at that spot like a dentist probing at a small area of decay. Go deep enough and you hit a nerve. Probe a millimeter deeper and you can put them screaming on their knees" (393). Thompson believes his players will be better for having been driven to their knees, but in fact they display the same wounds as the McCall brothers do in Beach Music, and just as Jack spends much of his adulthood alternately running from or trying to make sense of his damaged past, Mel Thompson's players spend decades denying their painful season under him even as they continue to relive its various injuries.[6]

Thompson's failures as a coach and as a surrogate father stem from his own unarticulated fear of becoming older in a society that privileges male potency. He is comfortable around his peers—he seems relaxed and even jovial when he is with other coaches and reporters, for instance—but he has no way of openly addressing his players, who are at once an extension of his own identity as a coach and simultaneously his rivals. Just as Don Conroy and his fictional doppelgänger Bull Meecham act out of a fear of being eclipsed by their sons, Thompson desperately tries to stave off evidence of his own decline by discouraging—and even fettering—his players. Conroy notes that Thompson only begins to pick on him when he is in the starting lineup, the Bulldogs' "Blue Team." He has been relatively anonymous to his coach as a "Green Weenie," a member of the second string, but when he is identified as a starter, "something in Mel's subconscious . . . stirred into life and the athlete that still lived within him became competitive" with Conroy (218). At the season's close, Thompson acknowledges this truth himself, although it is unclear if he fully understands its import. In what he may imagine to be a compliment, he tells Danny Mohr, who is the team's best shooter but has been repeatedly benched without explanation, "I've always been jealous of people who had more talent than I had" (345).

Perhaps the most damning evidence of Thompson's narcissism and insecurity, however, comes when Conroy visits him as part of the research process for *My Losing Season*. Conroy has already met with each of his former teammates, and they have shared their often-painful memories of each game they played under Thompson, recalled many of the practices he ran, and recounted even minor interactions with him as a way of searching for meaningful patterns and explanations. Unlike Conroy and his teammates, however, Thompson seems to recall nothing of the season and becomes animated only when discussing his own time as a player. There is a stark contrast between guard John De-Brosse, who tells Conroy without irony that the Bulldogs' last matchup with the University of Richmond "partially ruined my life," and Thompson, who seems untouched by that game and indeed by the season as a whole (9). In a canon defined by dreadful fathers, Thompson stands out as among the most irredeemable of father figures, unwilling to give of himself when he is needed and incapable of the kind of reflection that would allow for reconciliation.

Significantly, though, while he finds himself alternately humiliated, angered, and confounded by Thompson throughout the year, when Thompson is fired at the end of the season, Conroy writes a thirteen-page letter to the local newspaper protesting his dismissal, and when he meets up with Thompson to interview him as a part of his research for *My Losing Season,* he tells him, "I loved having you as my coach" (365). It is a paradox that can be frustrating— one reviewer wrote, "It leads you to wonder if the author has read his own book"—but it is also a contradiction that makes great sense in the context of Conroy's oeuvre.[7] As Conroy himself observes in *My Losing Season,* "In my life thus far there was nothing odd about this; love had always issued out of the places that hurt the most, and I feared few men as I feared Mel Thompson" (177). Mel, he confirms here, is simply another version of Don, and thus Conroy seems eternally locked in the role of a son desperately seeking acknowledgement from a father who is unwilling to give it.

Yet even as Conroy seems to affirm the inevitability of a brutal father-son dynamic that he has chronicled since *The Great Santini,* he also undermines such a reading in a series of scenes in which the paternal authority associated with basketball collides with the power of authorship; the result is a set of inversions, reversals, and disruptions that complicate the narrative in unexpected ways. Throughout *My Losing Season,* we are aware of the fact that Conroy's final year as a basketball player coincides with his birth as a writer. As the year begins, his conception of himself as an athlete and as an author are tentatively linked when he confesses to a station wagon full of baseball players that he plans to become a writer after he graduates, and we see these identities exist in clearer balance by the season's conclusion: in a bit of uncalculated symbolism, at the Citadel's end-of-year awards ceremonies, Conroy wins two trophies for his accomplishments on the basketball court and two medals for his literary work. In between these moments, we see him honing his creative skills in the same ways that he might practice a jump shot. When he is condemned to the bench alongside the Green Weenies, for instance, he finds himself assigning detailed fictional histories to interesting faces he spots in the stands, and when the team plays in New Orleans, he explores "the backstreets of the Vieux Carré the way I thought a writer might" (188).

The moment in which Conroy finds his true voice as a writer, however, is when he actively defies Thompson, whose most often repeated instruction to Conroy over the course of the season is the fairly discouraging order "Don't shoot!" After weeks of reluctant obedience, he finds his coach overridden by a voice in his head, one that urges him to "tune Mel out. Play the game because you love it. . . . Get yourself back" (217). He explicitly identifies this "breathtakingly assur[ed]" voice as "my writer's voice, the one that would come to me when I sat down to write my books." As interesting, however, is the fact that he also recognizes that "this interior voice . . . sounded much like that of my father" (217). The voice returns three times, and with each occurrence Conroy is baffled that it takes the form of "my father's voice, a voice I had loathed since childhood" (231). In an unexpected act of inversion, then, the voice that represents his authorial power and that urges him to resist paternal authority is also Don Conroy's voice.

The first time he hears the voice, Conroy drolly reports that he is more concerned that it may be a sign of schizophrenia than he is about what it reveals to him about his sense of self or his relationship with his father, and this dismissal is repeated in the narrative itself, which never fully explores the voice's significance. We might posit, however, that the appearance of this mysteriously hybridized voice—one that joins Conroy to his father and that represents both Conroy's athletic and authorial confidence—is crucial to the memoir. Most obviously the voice is nothing short of transformative. Conroy writes that "once I began believing in myself and not listening to the people who did not believe in me, I turned myself into a point guard who you needed to watch" (398). This confidence is replicated in his approach to writing, and he explains that "I came to the writing life as a point guard, and it became the metaphor of my transition. The novelist needs a strong ego, a sense of arrogance, complete knowledge of tempo, and control of the court" (399)[8].

As significant, however, is the fact that the voice also transforms Don Conroy. In linking the encouragement given by his inner voice to his father, Conroy creates the supportive father he has always wanted, one who does not humiliate and berate him but encourages him to have faith in his own abilities and instincts. This invented father becomes a real one in one of the great twists in Conroy's life and, more specifically, in *My Losing Season:* in the final chapters of the memoir, he reports that Don has "had the best second act in the history of fathering" (392) and has re-created himself as a more even-tempered, engaged parent. Interestingly this change is the direct result of the "writer's voice" that Don has unconsciously helped to create: Conroy credits Don's near-miraculous turnaround to the publication of *The Great Santini* in 1976, explaining that Don was so injured by the portrait of himself in the novel that he "remade himself and walked into his new life that I had willed and made possible for him" (392). We might argue, however, that Conroy willed and made possible this life long before he wrote *The Great Santini* and that the invention of their shared voice was, in fact, Conroy's first authorial creation.

In a wonderful moment of overturn, this voice is actualized within the narrative. At the end of the memoir, Conroy relays a conversation with Don that takes place in 1998, thirty years after the events he chronicles in *My Losing Season.* Speaking about Conroy's work, Don adopts a posture that is identical to the one he takes when haranguing his son after basketball games: Conroy reports that he is functioning in a state of "full-pitched fury" and is "red-faced and enraged" as he speaks, pointing forcefully at Conroy in an act of unconscious menace. Yet in this exchange he does not criticize Conroy; instead he tells him, "You're my son and you get it in your goddamn noggin that you're the best writer that ever lived. You got it, pal?" (391). Three decades after he has imagined it, Conroy's inner voice and Don's voice merge in a way that seems impossible earlier in the narrative.

This sort of revisionist, intertextual reading is openly invited by *My Losing Season* and, in fact, is indulged in the book as Conroy revisits experiences that he has previously explored in his fiction. He acknowledges that "fact and fiction have been engaged in an abnormal and fanciful dance since I first began my writing career" (291), but perhaps nowhere is this seen more clearly than in *My Losing Season.* In providing a sense of his life as a Citadel cadet in the memoir, for example, he recalls events that are recognizable as Will McLean's experiences in *The Lords of Discipline,* and in characterizing his early relationship with his father, he reprises fictional exchanges from *The Great Santini,* this time as fact.[9] This sense of fluidity between fact and fiction is most dramatic, however, in a chapter that recounts a series of overtimes in the Citadel's game against VMI, from which the Bulldogs emerge victorious after Conroy has made the successful final shots. He identifies the sinking of the last two-pointer as "the happiest, most fabulous moment of my life" (300), and this experience is replicated almost identically in *The Lords of Discipline,* where the glory is awarded to Will.

The chapter is not simply a retelling of the events that Conroy has previously dramatized, however. Instead it becomes a conversation between Conroy and a physical manifestation of Will. Defying the more conventional tone of the rest of the memoir, the chapter adopts an unexpectedly postmodern self-consciousness when Will, still a college senior, appears just as Conroy prepares to recall the triumphant game against VMI. In their imagined conversation, Will says he is about to play the game, but Conroy argues that he wants to "remember it accurately" and explains that Will, who is "something like" Conroy "but not completely," will corrupt his memory (292–93). The two have a brief standoff in which Conroy considers "eras[ing] Will McLean from the world" as a way of ensuring that his own history is not usurped by him, but ultimately Will defers, noting, "It's odd being fictional" (293). This rapprochement is not a full resolution, however, and the complexity of their relationship is further underscored by fact that Conroy has difficulty defining it: even as he recognizes Will as a fictionalized version of himself, he also introduces himself to Will as "your father" (292). In momentarily allowing his competing roles as creator and invention to coexist on the page, Conroy illuminates the slippages between lived experience and fictional remembrance that burden his work as both a novelist and memoirist, and the chapter suggests the existence of an ongoing extratextual conversation between these competing selves.

Memory is considered from another perspective in a second chapter that closely mirrors its fictional antecedent, this one dedicated to Conroy's romance with the young pregnant woman who served as the model for Will's first love in *The Lords of Discipline,* "Annie Kate." (Conroy underscores the fuzzy lines between fact and fiction by employing the same name he gave to Will's clandestine girlfriend as a pseudonym for the young woman with whom he actually fell in love.) In both the novel and Conroy's autobiographical account, Annie Kate dumps her earnest paramour after her pregnancy ends in stillbirth, and the heartbreak she causes scars both Conroy and his fictional doppelgänger. Conroy's recollection of his unconventional courtship of Annie Kate is a compelling story, and it provides his readership with a fascinating glimpse into the ways his experiences are reworked in his fiction. But the chapter is also an uneasy fit within the larger narrative of the memoir to some extent; for the most part, it falls outside the obvious temporal and thematic scope of *My Losing Season,* and, unlike *The Lords of Discipline,* where Annie Kate's loss haunts the narrative, Conroy never revisits the relationship after the end of the chapter devoted to her.

Yet while Annie Kate's story is not fully integrated into the memoir, the themes Conroy introduces in this chapter subtly inform his understanding of the complex nature of memory, and it is particularly useful in considering the players' response to their brutal 1966–67 season. Throughout *My Losing Season,* the idea of memory becomes a point of preoccupation for Conroy. He openly worries that his memories of some of the experiences that he presents as fact have become warped by time, and to counterbalance these fears—and perhaps to assuage the potential skepticism of his readers—he buttresses his stories with regular quotations from newspaper accounts of the Bulldogs' games and includes the observations of his teammates, all of whom he interviewed extensively—and often repeatedly.[10] Yet while his concern that he may have reshaped his memories is genuine, Conroy is more interested in the ways that memory shapes identity. At the conclusion of *My Losing Season,* he identifies the memoir as a project of "recovery" (394), a term that suggests the reclamation of lost stories. There are larger recoveries that are associated with memory, however: Conroy's relentless pursuit of the past has brought the team together after decades of separation, and they not only work to construct a collective narrative of their experience during the 1966–67 season, but they also renew their connections with one another. No less important, in sifting through his teammates' and his own memories, Conroy has initiated his own personal recovery. Before he began the project, he identifies himself as both "enclosed . . . in a shell of edgy despondency" after his divorce from Lenore and depleted by the emotional demands of writing *Beach Music* (12), but the act of researching and writing *My Losing Season* allows him to emerge with a more complete sense of self.

Given the obvious rewards of recalling even a difficult past, Conroy finds himself returning to the question of why all the members of the team would stubbornly refuse to remember the season or to recognize their roles in one another's lives. Early in the memoir he asserts, "It is the winners who have reunions," and he explains that "the names and faces of our teammates nick us like razors and recall moments of failure, disillusionment, disgrace" (6). These moments of disappointment—missed baskets, demoralizing practices, and benched games—are explored in detail throughout the narrative, but it is Annie Kate who, in responding to her own experience of an unwanted pregnancy, is able to clarify the players' response to the season. Just as she breaks up with Conroy in the wake of her pregnancy as a way of severing ties to the chief witness of her shame, his teammates seek to isolate themselves from one another so they will not be reminded of their own anguish.

Annie Kate's withdrawal from Conroy is shaded more subtly, however, in the explanation she gives him for leaving him: "You loved me when I hated myself" (258). Here she suggests that not only does Conroy serve as a reminder of her suffering, but his acceptance of her during this period—indeed his deep love for her—also suggests that her most authentic self was revealed during her pregnancy. Annie Kate seeks to see this period in her life as an anomaly, one that is entirely inconsistent with who she really is. Conroy's love for her complicates the narrative she has constructed for her own survival, and she is compelled to excise him from her life. Similarly Conroy's teammates hide from one another in their adulthoods not simply because they wish to avoid confronting the facts of their painful season, but because they understand that they have been fully known by their teammates during the period in which they too each hated themselves. To maintain contact with one another is to recognize the pain they experienced that season not as a form of isolated—and perhaps even unfortunate—suffering but, instead, as central to themselves.

Annie Kate's significance in the narrative continues in that she serves as an oblique form of cautionary tale. Conroy relates to us that he remains in contact with her but that their friendship is an odd one: "We did not discuss the thing that burned most brightly between us. I never once mentioned the ecstasy of my love for her and Annie Kate never once mentioned the baby. I still do not know if she ever read *The Lords of Discipline* or not, and she knows I will never ask that question" (249). Their relationship exists only in the context of détente, and thus while Conroy identifies it as "important to both of us," it is also "shallow, brittle, and lacks intimacy" (249). When he seeks out his teammates to relive their lost season, he is seeking a more authentic, and thus satisfying, connection. While he never makes reference to Annie Kate as he details his conversations with his teammates, the limited value of the polite fictions that define their adult relationship seems to inform his search for harder truths, even when they contain judgments that are painful to him.

We see this truth—and its ability to bruise—most clearly when Conroy meets with former center Al Kroboth and his wife, Patty. At Conroy's urging Kroboth speaks about his experiences as a prisoner of war in Vietnam, and while, as critic Jeff Turrentine noted, *My Losing Season* often "reads like a war memoir" in its descriptions of the Bulldogs' games,[11] when Conroy relays Kroboth's narrative, the tone of the book shifts dramatically to accommodate the actual battlefields that were a reality for many Citadel cadets after their graduation. Indeed in these pages basketball becomes invisible, and Conroy focuses on larger legacies—Kroboth's as a POW and Conroy's as an antiwar protestor. In the light of Kroboth's undeniable heroism, Conroy finds that he is once again compelled to reassess his own role in the war, and he writes that "I wish that I had entered into the Marine Corps and led a platoon of Marines in Vietnam. . . . Now I understood I should have protested the war after my return from Vietnam, after I had done my duty. I have come to a conclusion about my country that I knew then in my bones, but lacked the courage to act on: America is a good enough country to die for even when she is wrong" (376).Conroy gives this epiphany to Jordan Elliott in *Beach Music,* and Jordan's reconsideration of his stance toward the war in that novel suggests his deep need for formal atonement.[12] Similarly in passing a "harrowing, remorseless judgment" (377) on himself in *My Losing Season,* Conroy engages in a cathartic exercise that is a dramatic articulation of the memoir's larger project, one that may allow for the same promise of reparation and reinvention granted to Jordan.

Certainly Conroy cannot change the decisions he has made about the war, but he can address his broader fear that he has not become "the kind of man America can point to and say, 'There. That's the guy. . . . The one I can depend on'" (377) by ensuring, at least, that he is "that guy" for his teammates in their middle age. This role has long seemed elusive: as a point guard, he was the team's de facto strategist on the court, but his sense of himself as a leader had been regularly undermined by Mel Thompson. The coach had refused to name a team captain for the season, as is common practice, and instead identified an acting captain just moments before the start of each game. Thus while Conroy served as the captain for much of the season, he was never officially anointed by Thompson, and the role felt provisional and, at times, unearned. Given the instability Thompson created, the team never fully coalesced in the ways they might have, and Conroy notes that "in the locker room, you felt everything except what it was like to be part of a team" (35). As an adult, however, he is free to shake off the anxieties Thompson has instilled in him and to serve the team more fully. In the memoir's concluding pages, Conroy writes, "I found my team again, and they were in bad shape. I brought them together and I apologized to all of them. Not one of them knew how much I had loved and respected them when I was a young man disguised as the would-be captain of their team. . . . I got dizzy from loving that team, and I never told them" (400).

This scene—one in which the men affirm their affection for and connection with one another—echoes another exchange that Conroy recalls from his plebe year. He recounts a brutal episode of hazing designed to drive him from the Citadel after he wrote a poem mocking upperclassmen. The scene is familiar as Will McLean's experience in *The Lords of Discipline,* but it takes on a new resonance when Conroy claims it in *My Losing Season.* He recalls the hazing as his "lowest moment as a brother and ruined plebe" (116), but he then recalls the sense of almost miraculous communion he felt in its aftermath when he was embraced by his classmates. In the memoir he names each of the cadets who

come to his room to "offer words of encouragement and solidarity, and to ask
me to stay," and he recognizes that "my classmates came and left me a gift in
their wake—they sealed forever my desire to be one of them" (117). In collecting his teammates almost thirty years after the end of their season together and
offering them "words of encouragement and solidarity," Conroy replicates this
experience and thus cements their connection in a profound and lasting way.

The conclusion of *My Losing Season* is thus unabashedly optimistic. In the
preface to the memoir, Conroy writes that "I have a history of cracking up at
least once during the writing of each of my last five books" (13), but the tone
of the epilogue suggests restoration rather than collapse. In the final chapter,
which Conroy titles "New Game," we see the players engaged in a reunion, one
made even more meaningful to Conroy in that his father is in attendance as
well as Sandra King, whom he married the following year. In this way the past,
present, and future are joined for Conroy with a conclusiveness that might have
been savaged by the critics had *My Losing Season* been a work of fiction; as an
act of memoir, though, it seems a remarkable reward for the risk of probing a
painful past.

There is a second, even more unlikely, resolution at the end of *My Losing
Season* as well. After the Citadel's unrelentingly rancorous treatment of the
school's first female cadet, Shannon Faulkner, in 1995—a woman whose cause
Conroy had championed—the school became an object of public censure. Conroy reports that his father called and told him, "The Citadel needs you now,
son. It's in a free fall" (387), and after a series of tentative overtures from each
side, he accepted an invitation give the commencement speech in 2001. As part
of his agreement, though, he insisted that Lt. Col. Nugent Courvoisie, "the
Boo," and Al Kroboth also accompany him and be recognized. In resolving his
own uneasy relationship with the school, Conroy was also able to redress symbolically the wrongs the Citadel had done to the Boo, thus closing the circle created by *The Boo* and *The Lords of Discipline*. Moreover he was able to affirm
publicly his admiration for and gratitude to Kroboth—and by extension their
classmates who had served in Vietnam—to a Citadel audience, an important
act of reparation for Conroy. When he writes about the event in *My Losing Season*, it is devoid of the ambivalence he usually displays for the school; instead
he acknowledges that the Citadel has shaped him personally and inspired him
artistically and notes with genuine delight that he too has shaped the school:
he is reminded of own impact not only by the Boo's presence but the winking
salute he is given by a female cadet. In this way *My Losing Season*'s focus on
Conroy's college basketball career broadens to include, and to expand upon,
the themes that have defined his writing life, and the memoir, which he had

initially worried would derail his career, instead functions as a capstone of his work until this point.

Conroy's next project, *The Pat Conroy Cookbook: Recipes and Stories of My Life* (2004), is a much more whimsical act of autobiography. The book is at once a useful collection of recipes and a compilation of vignettes, some of which are introspective in nature and others that substantiate his reputation as a delightful raconteur. (Conroy is famously at odds with his Irish heritage, but his cookbook is among the clearest evidence that "he is great craic," as the Irish say of their best storytellers.) Conroy has said of the project, "I never enjoyed writing anything more. All I did was remember how I was introduced to all these recipes, whether through my Italian roommates from college, or my Orlando aunt with her coconut cake," and indeed there is often a sense of joy and playfulness about the collection, which moves easily among the various phases of his life and that follows him in his many travels.[13] Conroy includes recipes and stories that are rooted in his childhood, those that he discovered as a self-trained cook, and even those that he has encountered in the work of talented and inventive chefs.

In this way *The Pat Conroy Cookbook* is an interesting anomaly. Conroy published the book during a period of renewed interest in food as a lens for reinterpreting regional culture; in 1997 *The New Encyclopedia of Southern Culture* added a volume devoted to southern foodways, for example, and in 1999 a group of academics formed the Southern Foodways Alliance, and their work has helped to shape the field of southern studies in the intervening years.[14] In its treatment of southern barbeque, corn pudding, and homemade mayonnaise, for instance, *The Pat Conroy Cookbook* certainly offers the kind of insight into regional history and culture that is at the heart of such projects, but Conroy refuses to elevate southern comfort food above the other cuisines that have made an impact on him, a fact he signals in the cookbook's introduction when he notes that he was not taught to cook by his mother—defying the oral tradition associated with southern cooking—but learned by studying Auguste Escoffier's *Le Guide Culinaire,* a cookbook known for "impos[ing] intellectual order on the classical kitchen" and ushering in the era of modern gastronomy.[15] Elsewhere in the introduction, Conroy promises to "write of truffles in the Dordogne Valley in France, cilantro in Bangkok, catfish in Alabama, scuppernong in South Carolina, Chinese food from my years in San Francisco, and white asparagus from the first meal my agent, Julian Bach, took me to in New York City" (6). In short he does not hew to a fashionable construction of "down-home" cooking, which employs food to honor tradition and reify identity, and instead he frees food from these constraints, identifying "the love of cooking [as] a portable, moveable pleasure" (4). Moreover Conroy's collection of stories and recipes suggest that one that can draw from a diverse—and perhaps unconventional—set of histories and traditions.

The Pat Conroy Cookbook also addresses the connection between food and literature more explicitly. When visiting New Orleans for the first time with the Citadel basketball team, an event he recounts in *My Losing Season,* Conroy sees food as a physical manifestation of the imaginative satisfaction of reading. He writes that "I stood before Antoine's and Brennan's and I breathed in the air that floated like clouds out of those restaurants, perfumed with garlic and the brine of oysters and the great brown pungency of sirloins. Someday, I promised myself, I would return to these restaurants and sit myself beneath the diamond-backed light of chandeliers and order all the meals I had read about in books but had never eaten. People would eat well and drink well in my books, I thought" (188). The meals Conroy provides his characters in *The Prince of Tides* and *Beach Music,* most specifically, are indeed magnificent, and food offers an important expression of the emotions that are otherwise inarticulable for his characters; the generosity that is implied in its preparation or the sympathy that is conveyed in its ordering allows characters a way of connecting authentically with one another. In the stories contained in *The Pat Conroy Cookbook,* food similarly becomes a way of better understanding those who have prepared dishes for and with Conroy, and meals become acts of small communion. The careful instructions Conroy provides for the recipes that follow each vignette are a practical necessity of any cookbook, but they also complete this cycle; he not only shares the personal significance of each dish with his reader but also invites them to participate in its creation and consumption.

CHAPTER 8

South of Broad

After the publication of *My Losing Season* and *The Pat Conroy Cookbook*, *South of Broad* (2009) marked a return to form for Conroy: it is an epic novel, one that is grounded in the familiar landscape of the South Carolina lowcountry and shaped by the intricate domestic politics and dramatic narrative twists that are hallmarks of his work. *South of Broad*'s title references one of Charleston's most elegant neighborhoods, an area that has become synonymous with the city's deep history and aristocratic graciousness, and as its selection suggests, the novel is interested in exploring the psychic terrain of this community, carefully mapping its various literal, spiritual, and social architectures. There is also a certain irony to the geographical specificity of the novel's title, however, in that *South of Broad* expands beyond the borders it celebrates literally—much of its central action takes place in San Francisco—and metaphorically: its characters often find that they do not fit easily into Charleston's strict social hierarchies. *South of Broad* becomes not just a consideration of Charleston's most insular and venerated culture but also an examination of the ways in which the cultural boundaries of the South are shifting.

While *South of Broad* is marked by a tighter temporal focus than *Beach Music*, the novel that precedes it, it is shaped by a plot that is equally ambitious. The novel opens just before protagonist Leo King's senior year of high school, and we learn that Leo is struggling to create a "normal" life after the suicide of his brother, Steve, an event that took place ten years earlier. Leo's life has been largely derailed since he discovered Steve with his wrists slit; in the immediate aftermath of his brother's suicide, he suffers a breakdown he identifies as "the Great Drift" and is institutionalized (4). Even after he is deemed healed, however, he seems unable to find his bearings; used to following "a path" that "Steve cleared," Leo continues to drift in many ways (4). He is ultimately put on probation when he is arrested for a crime he did not commit: when a party he is attending is raided, an older boy whom Steve had admired plants drugs on him, and Leo accepts the guilt as his own. In *South of Broad*'s early pages, Leo simultaneously appears to be touchingly naive and tragically wise, finding meaning primarily in his obligations as an altar boy, a paperboy, and an assistant in an antique shop, roles that provide him with a well-defined, if lonely, path in Steve's absence.

As Leo is finishing the requirements of his legal probation, though, he is also coming to the end of what might be seen as an emotional probationary period, and in a single day, he is transformed from a "timid boy" to one who exists at the center of a group of ten friends, a coterie that will persist into adulthood (9). Leo meets each of these new friends as he runs a series of errands for his mother, and the rapid-fire nature of these connections, which might otherwise be considered unlikely, is explained by the fact that they occur on June 16, the same day on which James Joyce's *Ulysses* is set, celebrated by Joyce's fans as Bloomsday. Leo loosely echoes the wanderings of Joyce's protagonist, Leopold Bloom, as he crisscrosses Charleston at his mother's bequest, and just as Bloom encounters a series of disparate characters in Dublin, Leo assembles a group of diverse friends in Charleston: Starla and Niles Whitehead are orphans from the North Carolina mountains; Sheba and Trevor Poe are charismatic twins who have moved in across the street from the Kings; Ike Jefferson is a football player who has reluctantly followed his father to Leo's high school, Peninsula, where the elder Jefferson will be the first black coach; and Molly Huger and Chad Rutledge are South of Broad bluebloods who have been kicked out of their private school and thus will attend Peninsula for their senior year. The group is rounded out by Chad's sister, Fraser, and Betty Roberts, who befriends Niles and Starla at the orphanage.

The themes of *Ulysses* continue to be evident in *South of Broad*, and Conroy sprinkles his novel with moments of intertextual play, but for the most part *South of Broad*'s plot is defined by rhythms more in keeping with Conroy's oeuvre than Joyce's.[1] The novel unfolds as the group coalesces in their senior year of high school, finding points of connection with one another and, as often, wounding one another as they seek to negotiate the landmines of race and class that lie just below the surface of their evolving friendships. When the novel jumps ahead twenty years—from 1969 to 1989—these tensions persist, but the passage of time has cemented the group's ties. Most obviously their connections are solidified by marriage—Ike and Betty have married one another, as have Niles and Fraser, Chad and Molly, and Leo and Starla—but they also remain committed to one another through their shared friendship. This is seen most clearly when Sheba, now a movie star, returns to Charleston to enlist their coterie in a search for Trevor, who is rumored to be suffering from AIDS and is believed to have slipped into the underbelly of San Francisco to die in anonymity. In an act of affirmation, the group travels to California to help locate Trevor, an already intimidating quest that is rendered terrifying when they realize that they are being followed by the Poe twins' father, a sexual predator and serial killer who is obsessed with his children. The novel ends with the sort of dramatic plot twists that also mark the conclusions of *The Prince of Tides* and *Beach Music:* while Trevor is saved as the result of the group's collective bravery, Sheba is killed by her father in an act of unfathomable brutality, and this loss is paralleled by the destruction of much of Charleston by Hurricane Hugo.

Reviewers were quick to take issue with *South of Broad*'s dramatic plot lines, yet like Conroy's earlier work, the novel's most sensational plot points are regularly eclipsed by the domestic narratives that lie at its heart; even as *South of Broad* traces its characters' often-outsized exploits, the novel reflects Conroy's continuing fascination with the complex dynamics that shape families, both those that are biologically defined and those that are conceived through friendship and marriage.[2] While it represents a return to these themes, though, *South of Broad* also makes a significant—and even startling—break with Conroy's previous work in that Leo's father, Jasper King, is a quietly generous and instinctively kind man. Conroy has explained this fairly extraordinary shift by noting, "I always needed [a good father] so I created one," and indeed Jasper King is an exemplary parent.[3] Unlike the fathers who terrorize their sons elsewhere in Conroy's work, Jasper is defined by his great sympathy for Leo, and he is as wounded by his son's essential loneliness as Leo is himself. A science teacher by profession, Jasper becomes Leo's teacher, mentor, and model, and throughout the novel we see Jasper sharing his own skills with Leo—he teaches Leo to fish and to cook, for instance—but also providing essential affirmation of Leo's successes: in a particularly resonant ceremony of recognition, for instance, he toasts to Leo's manhood in a ritual passed on from his own father, and less formally, Jasper regularly confirms Leo's manhood through his simple assumption of it. When the Poe house is broken into early in the novel, for example, he wakes Leo and tells him simply, "There's trouble across the street" (98). They form a two-man posse, and while their search does not result in the capture of a suspect, it silently confirms Jasper's faith in Leo's bravery and integrity. Leo succinctly sums up his relationship with his father when he notes, "He was more North Star than father" (3).

Jasper's influence continues to guide Leo even after his untimely death, as is evinced in a series of parallel scenes in which he first models a behavior and then Leo, in his father's absence, unconsciously mimics it. The first of these occurs when, as a high school student, Leo finds Harrington Canon, the cantankerous owner of the antique store where Leo works, confined to his bed and covered in his own blood and excrement. Leo instinctively begins to care for Mr. Canon, cleaning him, preparing food for him, and calling his doctor. He then calls Jasper, who responds by saying, "I'm there, son. Right now. You and Mr. Canon hold on, and we'll get this thing done right" (355). After Mr. Canon has been taken to the hospital, Jasper and Leo clean his house, eliminating the physical evidence of his suffering in an act that is both intimate and arduous. Mr. Canon dies before he can return to his house and witness their handiwork, but when Leo is visiting him in the hospital he tells Mr. Canon that Jasper has explained to him that they were obligated to undertake the task because they "were the only two people in a position to do anything" (364).

Twenty years later this scene is reenacted when Sheba brings Leo and his friends to San Francisco to search for Trevor. As part of their search, the group brings meals to AIDS patients who have rented rooms in dingy hotels as they prepare for their deaths, and when Leo enters one room he finds that its occupant, a beautiful young man, has died. While his instinct is to "run away from the presence of this dead . . . boy," instead Leo strips the young man's soiled bed, cleans and perfumes his body, and shaves his face (265). There is a religious quality to the rituals he performs, but they also closely echo the duties Jasper models for him when he finds Mr. Canon. Once again the tasks Leo undertakes are both physically and emotionally difficult, and the results remain invisible to their beneficiary. Leo's commitment to performing them reveals the ways he has inherited Jasper's profound sense of obligation to "get this thing done right" and his belief that acts of human kindness—even when unacknowledged—should be undertaken by those "in a position to do something."

Leo's larger decision to look for Trevor Poe is also shaped by his father's model. When Leo is in high school, he learns that Chad Rutledge has nominated Trevor and Niles Whitehead, one of the orphans, for membership in one of Charleston's most exclusive fraternities, the Middleton Assembly. The nomination is a sham, however, and the two have been invited to the induction ceremony merely so they can be shamed before the club's members in an act of particularly cruel theater. The experience becomes exceptionally painful for Niles when, in a moment that is as casual as it is callous, the club members reveal that his mother and grandmother have died, a fact of which Niles had been unaware. He and his sister, Starla, have held on to the belief that they would be rescued from their lives as orphans as soon as their family could locate them, and so the news—delivered as part of a larger rebuke—is devastating. In response to the new hopelessness of his situation and in a desperate attempt to connect himself to a home that is now evacuated of meaning, Niles flees to his family's abandoned homestead deep in the North Carolina mountains.

When Jasper hears the story, he says simply, "Leo, a field trip to the mountains tomorrow. You're going to bring Niles back" (386). In its patent minimalism, Jasper's order confirms Leo's authority and obligation, but more importantly, it redefines Niles and Starla's sense of home. The Whitehead siblings' identity as orphans has meant that any construction of home is inherently temporary. In insisting that Niles needs to be brought home to Charleston, however, Jasper forcefully erases their placelessness and claims Niles and Starla in an act that subverts the Middleton Assembly's dismissal of them. Similarly when Leo accepts Sheba's proposal to find Trevor in San Francisco, he echoes Jasper's rhetoric, explaining, "We're going to bring [Trevor] home" (224). In fact Trevor has only lived in Charleston for a single year, and thus in this statement Leo is acknowledging the ways in which the group's friendship grounds them in a common home, just as Jasper has done. Less obviously, in replicating the overture that his father has made to the Whiteheads, Leo similarly mitigates the sense of marginalization that Trevor experiences because of his ambiguous origins—his mother is recognized as a "common drunk" (383)—and, more significantly, his open homosexuality, an anomaly in the South in that period.

If Jasper instills Leo with a sense of himself as tied to family—both biological and created—Leo's mother is a more intimidating, more alienating figure. Lindsay King is all hard angles and edges, and her speech is often stiff and humorless. She is an administrator to Jasper's teacher—she is, in fact, the principal of Leo's high school—and where Jasper finds himself in awe of the wonder of nature, "pray[ing] to [it] because it was his synonym for God" (3), Lindsay is a strict Catholic who seeks comfort in the rituals and demands of daily mass. Lindsay is a devotee of James Joyce, and she has not only published "unreadable" essays on his work but has named both of her children after his major characters: Steve's full name is Stephen Dedalus King, and Leo's name is Leopold Bloom King (20). There is an obvious irony in this enthusiasm: most immediately, Leo has not enjoyed his early encounters with *Ulysses*, and so he cannot understand his namesake. Indeed he feels as if he has been robbed of a more fitting patrimony, suggesting, "You could've named me after my father! I'd have liked that" (35). The name is unsuitable not only in its inability to convey a meaningful legacy, but also in its failure to capture Leo's personality: Leo—suggesting of a lion—is inconsistent with Leo's tentative and obedient nature, and Bloom seems a mockery of the fact that Leo has "turned out to be a late bloomer" (5). Lindsay is largely untroubled by these incongruities, however; while she seems disappointed in Leo's lack of appreciation of *Ulysses*, she seems equally happy to claim Joyce as a personal passion, accepting Jasper's identification of Bloomsday as "your day," for example (22).

Just as Lindsay is closely aligned with a text that is unreadable to Leo, she herself remains mysterious to him, adopting an identity that is simultaneously fluid and obscured. When he addresses her about school matters, for example, she demands that Leo refer to her as "Dr. King," a move designed to signal the official nature of their conversation, but one that also serves to erase her maternal identity. More dramatically Leo learns that prior to her marriage to Jasper, Lindsay had been a nun and had taken the name "Sister Norberta." Thus the woman Leo identifies as Lindsay is also Norberta, and his mother is also "sister." As a result he feels not only that he does not know his mother, but also that he cannot know himself; after his discovery of his mother's history, he thinks to himself, "A week ago, I would have written out my autobiography and not even come close to approaching its central truth" (96). Interestingly Jasper tells Leo that Steve knew about Lindsay's life as a nun but that after his death they decided to "emphasize us as a family, not your mother's life before we married" (81). This expurgation of the past, ostensibly intended to render the family more secure, has potentially devastating consequences for Leo, however: just as Lindsay withholds her love from Leo in the wake of Steve's death—Sheba accuses Lindsay of "treat[ing] Leo like he was the second-place trophy you got for losing your golden boy" (164)—she refuses to share her history with him as she had with Steve, and thus she fails to help Leo to make sense of his own history.

Lindsay's essential remoteness is significant not only in the ways that it undermines Leo's sense of himself, but also in the fact that it accentuates Jasper's remarkable warmth and compassion. In fact in granting Jasper such marked powers of sympathy, maintained even in spite of his wife's iciness, Conroy risks creating a father who is "flawless, way too good to be true," the same criticism he expressed about one of his earliest creations, Lillian Meecham.[4] In fact, however, he subverts the ideal of the perfect father throughout the novel. Most obviously Jasper is an anomaly in a book filled with flawed—and even monstrous—fathers: Niles and Starla have been abandoned by their alcoholic, abusive father; Chad and Fraser's father, Chadworth Rutledge IX, is an entitled bigot who is unashamed of bullying those who possess less power than he does; and Niles and Sheba's father is a sociopath who has raped his children throughout their childhood and terrorized them throughout their adulthood. Equally horrific is the novel's symbolic father, Monsignor Max Sadler, who occupies a trusted position in the community and in the King family specifically: he helps Leo find a way back to his faith after Steve's suicide, tenderly recalls Jasper at his funeral, and serves as Lindsay's confidante, later paving the way for to her to rejoin the convent. Yet in the novel's conclusion, it is revealed that Monsignor Max raped

Steve, an act of physical, emotional, and spiritual violence that has driven Steve to commit suicide and consequently leads to Leo's despair. Jasper may be a good father, but certainly the role itself is a polluted one.

Moreover while the novel continually credits Jasper with reifying Leo's sense of home, it simultaneously demonstrates that Jasper's idealized form of home is out of step with Charlestonian identity and thus limited in the succor it provides. In the novel's opening page, Leo recalls that Jasper has nicknamed Charleston "the Mansion on the River," a lovely phrase that both bows to the city's beauty and recognizes Charleston's historic homes as a defining metonym for the city itself. Interestingly, however, when Jasper constructs his own house, Leo notes that "many Charlestonians considered [it] the ugliest house in the historical district" (34). Even more telling, though, is the house's description as "as functional and as homely as a Catholic church built in the Charleston suburbs of that era" (90), a fairly damning assessment in a book that venerates the indulgences of Charleston proper, and one that suggests the house's inability to inspire or reinforce faith. Thus while Jasper is "peacock proud of a town so pretty it makes your eyes ache with pleasure just to walk down its spellbinding, narrow streets" (1), he has built a house that is a blemish on its beauty and that stands in defiance of the qualities of Charleston he most adores. This incongruence hints at the ways in which in which Jasper is not "at home" in the city that is also "the great love of his life" (1).

Leo, also his father's creation, reflects many of the flaws evinced in the house Jasper King has built. He repeatedly refers to his unattractiveness throughout the novel, identifying his face as "off-centered" and "amphibian-like," and his self-assessment is reflected in the nickname he is given in school and that persists into adulthood, "Toad" (306). He notes that "to be born ugly in a city that prizes beauty . . . that's a real tragedy" (198), and his self-professed unattractiveness links him to the "homely" house that his father has designed and created. Just as the Kings' house separates them from aristocratic Charleston in its pronounced plainness and its dogged middle-classness, Leo, too, occupies a marginalized position in the city, and as he travels through the city on his paper route early each morning, he appears as both a supplicant to the city's beauty and a voyeur preoccupied with those who inhabit it with instinctive self-assurance. While Leo knows the details of Charleston's rhythms more intimately than many who were born South of Broad, the city only feels as if it is his in the early morning hours before it becomes fully alive. There is a fair irony, then, in his appreciation of the mansions that line Meeting Street as possessing "front doors heavy and sumptuous enough to be the entrances to the residences of kings" (14). Leo, of course, is a King but, as he knows all too well, not the sort for whom such doors are designed.

In an unexpected twist, however, Leo does inherit one of these mansions when Harrington Canon, his employer at the antique store, bequeaths his Tradd Street home to him after he dies of leukemia. Leo embraces the gift fully, and he sees the house as "a solid reminder that life could hurl good luck at you as easily as it could devastation or ruin" (453). Yet despite his genuine delight and pride in the house, there is a sense of illegitimacy to his inheritance, one that is voiced directly when Mr. Canon's "outraged but distant" (414) relatives contest the will and that is intimated more subtly in the bequest's innate violation of Charleston's natural order. As his father tells Leo, "South of Broad is a conspiracy of platelets, son: blood and breeding are all that matter there" (327). Leo, of course, is a product of "inferior" breeding, as his father's house attests, and he has no "blood" claim to his South of Broad inheritance. In his acceptance of Canon's mansion, then, he defies Charleston's expectations of succession.

Leo's uncertain position is further complicated by Mr. Canon's own problematic relationship to the "conspiracy of platelets" that shapes South of Broad. While as an antique dealer he is an authority on familial history, he also represents a complete rupture with the kind of patriarchal lineage that underlies the value of the objects he sells. He confesses to Leo that he has rejected a path that includes marriage and children because "I was a bitter disappointment to both my mother and father. An only child never outgrows that. That's a wound that suppurates through the years." As a result, he says, "I chose a reclusive life because it seemed to fit me best" (365). Mr. Canon represents a severance of his family line on both sides, one that Leo echoes in the fragile relationship he has with Lindsay after Jasper's death and in his own childlessness, a reflection of the larger barrenness of his marriage to Starla. (While Leo would desperately like to have children, Starla, who is irreparably damaged from her own violent and insecure childhood, aborts her pregnancies as a way of punishing him.) While Leo is not driven to the level of emotional sequestration that Mr. Canon seeks, he too has a fragile relationship with his mother and is without sibling, true partner, or heir (140).

Given these paradoxical economic and spiritual inheritances from his father and Mr. Canon, Leo seems destined to occupy a liminal position in hierarchical Charleston, a fact that is further evinced in his professional life. In a transition that echoes Leo's dramatic move from his middle-class childhood home to the mansion on Tradd Street, he has graduated from his position as a paperboy for the *News and Courier* to become the paper's most popular columnist. Just as his relocation to South of Broad does, on an immediate level Leo's column confirms his connection to, and heightened status within, the city he loves. The column is devoted to capturing Charleston's inner workings by relaying gossip about its most influential citizens and by sharing bits of local color and wisdom, a model exemplified by legendary *San Francisco Chronicle* columnist Herb Caen, a real figure who makes a cameo in the novel when he helps publicize the search for Trevor.[5] Trevor has identified Caen as "defin[ing] his city with wit, sophistication, and flair" (233), and Leo endeavors to do the same, translating the subtleties of the city's social politics for the uninitiated. Yet even though he is a professional "insider," Leo is also conscious of the fact that he does not fully participate in the world he chronicles. As he notes as a teenager, Charleston "was a city and club that knew exactly whom it wanted, and I didn't fit the bill in any of its particulars. And I was well aware of it" (46). As an adult he is still relegated to the role of guest in the city's most exclusive enclaves.

Leo's complex relationship to aristocratic Charleston is exemplified in his relationship with Molly Huger Rutledge.[6] When Leo first meets Molly, he notes that "there was nothing about [her] that was not a cliché to me," and in fact as a teenage boy who has only known her for a few minutes, he is able to predict her future with an impressive accuracy: "For the rest of her life, she could sit around being beautiful, marrying Chadworth the tenth and bearing his heirs, rising to the presidency of the Junior League, and putting fresh flowers on the altar of St. Michael's. With thoughtless ease she could throw parties for her husband's law firm, sit on the board of the Dock Street Theatre, and restore a mansion south of Broad" (53). Despite the inherent superficiality of the role Molly seems destined to embrace, however, Leo finds that when he considers her next to her obvious foil, Chad's sister, Fraser, a spirited basketball player who defies a clear role in Charlestonian typology, he discovers to his surprise that "I was much more attracted to Molly than to Fraser" (53), and indeed he remains quietly in love with Molly throughout his adulthood. While Leo and Molly share a genuine and easy intimacy, however, the clichés that Leo first associates with her are never fully eradicated; their friendship is continually informed by his belief that she "is one of the great beauties of her Charleston generation, and I am just a foot soldier in society who knows his place in the order of things" (269).

Indeed Molly seems to treat Leo as a loyal conscript when she briefly recasts their friendship as a romance, once in high school and again in adulthood. In the first instance, she invites him to a high school dance after Chad has broken up with her, and in the second she initiates sex with him shortly after Chad has been caught in one of his many affairs. These romantic overtures are short-lived, however, and after each episode she returns to Chad. As a result we may see Molly as a well-meaning but ultimately careless figure, one who seeks to bolster her self-esteem by turning to Leo when she feels most insecure and who dismisses him when she has recovered her bearings. Leo takes a more generous view of Molly, however. In part this is the result of his deep affection for her: when she abandons him after the high school dance to go home with Chad, for instance, Leo notes that "even in my disappointment, I couldn't bring myself to hate her. She was too vulnerable and too basically decent, in spite of what she'd done to me, for me to work up any great fury against her" (373).

Leo's acceptance of Molly's treatment of him is also deeply revealing of Charleston's complex social codes, however. When she abandons him during their high school date, for example, wordlessly slipping from his car to Chad's after Chad has been humiliated in a fight, Leo sees her as returning to "the place she was born to sit" (348). He requires no explanation or apology from her, and he continues to see her as "basically decent" in part because he is as invested in the hierarchies that separate them as she is. Similarly when she returns to Chad after her brief affair with Leo in their adulthood, she never tells him of her decision, allowing him to learn about the change in their relationship merely by offering him an expression that is "resigned and even a little comforted" (424). Leo can read this expression as clearly as if it were a detailed letter, however, and in fact he might be described as feeling the same way; he is resigned to the loss of Molly but comforted in an odd way that she has returned to "the life she was born to lead" (424). Leo's other relationships with women challenge Charleston's strict social codes: most obviously he marries Starla Whitehead, who as an orphan truly defies the ideal of both "breeding and blood," and he has a long-running flirtation with Sheba Poe, whose pronounced beauty and sex appeal make her an American commodity but place her outside of Charlestonian conventions. Yet his continued desire for Molly, a woman who is inseparable from her aristocratic status, is more lasting and more defining than his commitment to Starla or his attraction to Sheba, and it confirms and clarifies Leo's ambivalent relationship to Charleston's aristocracy.

South of Broad's examination of race closely parallels its consideration of class. The novel is notable in Conroy's canon in that in addition to its interest in the experience of the liberal white southerner who fights racial prejudice, often a trope in Conroy's work, it also seeks to consider African Americans' experiences more directly by giving black characters—specifically Ike and Betty—an expanded role in the text. Moreover while works like *The Great Santini* and *The Lords of Discipline* consider race in the context of the civil rights era, *South of Broad*'s wider scope allows this discussion to be extended into the late 1980s. Thus while the scenes of the novel that are set in 1969 reflect a racial dynamic that is familiar to Conroy's readers—Leo lends his authority to Ike on the football field and in a number of different social settings, for instance—in the scenes that take place in 1989, this dynamic has undergone a dramatic shift. Ike, significantly, is the city's first black chief of police, and Betty is also a police

officer. As a result not only do Ike and Betty not need to be "saved" by the liberal white South, but they also now protect Charleston, and in their uniforms
and badges, they are literally cloaked in authority.

Yet Conroy does not mean to suggest that racial prejudice has been eradicated, and in two scenes that stand in stark contrast to one another, he demonstrates the continuing—and perhaps increased—complexity of race in the
South. In the first scene, set in 1969, Wormy Ledbetter, "the *Tyrannosaurus rex*
of the classic southern redneck" (306), flings racial epithets at Ike and other
black classmates outside the high school. Leo, along with Niles, Trevor, and
Sheba, immediately intervenes, even though he knows he is risking an "ass-
whipping" from Wormy and the wrath of his mother, who as the school principal must dole out punishments after the incident (309). The second scene is
set twenty years later, and the group is assembled on a San Francisco cable car
as they set out to find Trevor. Sheba catches a man lifting her wallet out of her
purse and shouts, "Get your goddamn *black* hand out of my purse," and when
he tells her he cannot free himself because her purse is wrapped around his
wrist, she says, "Let go of my goddamned wallet and I'll loosen the purse, you
smelly black son of a bitch" (255). Leo, Niles, and Trevor are all present again,
but in this instance, in which the racist remarks come from a friend rather than
a "T. rex," none of them jump into action. Only Molly speaks up, mildly suggesting to Sheba, "I'd lose the references to smell and color" (255).

This collective silence is echoed by Ike and Betty, who have handcuffed the
man even though they lack jurisdictional authority. When he complains to
them, "You heard that woman call me a nigger. It was a racial incident, plain
and simple. I'm the victim of a hate crime," Betty simply says, "Shut up, mister.
Give us time to think" (255). The implication is that Betty and Ike are most
concerned with their own transgressions, but it is the collective acceptance of
Sheba's language that represents a greater violation. While she has not used the
word *nigger*, as the man claims, she has indeed perpetrated a "racial incident," a
fact underscored by her decision to employ "a drop-dead perfect Charleston accent" as she berates the man, a move "that only exacerbates the racial tension"
(256). Ultimately the situation is diffused when the group realizes that the man
who robbed Sheba grew up outside Charleston and, in fact, was the star player
for a rival high school. Their common history translates into a shared recognition of racial epistemologies, and the incident quietly dissolves in the narrative.

The marked disparity of these scenes—one that leads to confrontation and
the other that leads to erasure—underscores the fact that the diverse group of
friends Conroy has assembled is, on one hand, an embodiment of civil rights
ideals and, on the other, an illustration of a contemporary unwillingness—
or inability—to think critically about racism. When the group does talk about

race, their denunciations of white prejudice are almost universally focused
on the past—Betty jokes about the fact that "before I met you white folks in
high school, I thought all of you subscribed to the *Ku Klux Klan Weekly*," for
instance (173)—and when they touch on the realities of the present day, their
conversations are often vague and tinged with a wryness that suggests further
discussion is unnecessary. In one exchange, for instance, Leo says, "Race. At
least it's not complicated down South," and Betty agrees, "We always have that.
Complete ease and trust among my people and yours" (149). In Charleston
after the civil rights era, racial difference is treated much like class difference;
it can be mentioned glancingly, but the hierarchies that are dependent upon it
are viewed as inviolable and the injustices that result are seen as uncomfortable
realties.

This sense of social stasis is disrupted in *South of Broad*'s conclusion,
however, when Hurricane Hugo ravages Charleston. The storm destroys much
of the city, and its impact is felt both broadly and personally: Leo's childhood
home is filled with mud and, more dramatically, Molly's grandmother's home,
which had been a place of solace for Leo as well as Molly, is demolished by the
winds and waves. As Molly is grieving for this lost history, she spots a beached
porpoise, and she and Leo work together to get it back out to sea. Leo later
writes a column about their experience, positing that "by saving the porpoise,
Molly had saved something in the soul of Charleston" (467). Certainly the moment recalls the redemptive return of Snow to Colleton in *The Prince of Tides*,
but perhaps the "soul of Charleston" is more accurately saved by the hurricane
itself. Leo notes that Molly "made the amazing discovery that a palmetto is
more likely to survive a hurricane than a hundred-year-old oak tree. Her theory
is that the palmetto tree has more natural flexibility and can bend all the way to
the ground and still survive, but an oak knows only how to stand firm against
the amazing blasts of wind, and makes itself susceptible to the perils of uproot-
ing" (472). Similarly Charleston, too, is learning to bend. After the hurricane
Leo notes:

> [A] brand-new civilization has sprung alive on Church Street as a small
> nation of contractors and subcontractors begins a long and fruitful season
> of renewal and salvage. The interior of every house on the street hums with
> the concentrated activity of repairmen of every stripe. Painters and roofers
> stare out at me from high scaffolding as I pass them in the street below. A
> friendly city at the worst of times, Charleston's innate cordiality informs
> its sensibility after the disaster. People wave and shout greetings to one
> another, whether an apprentice carpenter or a descendent of a signer of the
> Declaration of Independence. (482)

In this "irrepressible resurrection," Charleston will make new histories where it cannot salvage the old, and the sort of snobbishness and latent racism that has defined its value system will have to give way to a system more reflective of its creators, those "painters and apprentice carpenters" (482) who are literally rebuilding the city alongside those who are traditionally viewed as the architects of its culture.

In its destructiveness, then, Hugo ushers in a new phase of Charleston's history, and *South of Broad* ends with a celebration of the cyclical, a theme that resonates in the conclusions of almost all of Conroy's work. The closing action of the novel occurs on Bloomsday, further signaling that we have returned to a point of origin, and like the city of Charleston, Leo is trying to repair—and, as importantly, re-create—himself. Just as Hugo has devastated the city, Leo has been shattered by the revelation that Monsignor Max molested Steve, a violation that is preceded by a number of significant losses: Starla has committed suicide, Sheba has been murdered by her father, and Lindsay has returned to the convent. Faced with such loss, Leo finds himself suicidal, and he is admitted to a psychiatric ward where he revisits his history in drug-influenced dreams. As Leo emerges from the deepest point of his depression, though, he is rewarded with a sign of renewal that is as striking as the porpoise Molly finds after Hugo: in his final days at the hospital, a nurse asks him out on a date. This sign is rendered even more auspicious when the nurse mentions to Leo that she has a son. Monsignor Max has died shortly after Leo learns of his crime, and Trevor and Sheba's father has drowned in the rising waters created by Hugo; as these monstrous fathers are expunged from his history, Leo has a chance to be reborn as the father he has always wanted to be.

In a bow to *Ulysses*, Conroy ends *South of Broad* with the word "Yes" (512), and as it does in Joyce's work, this sincere affirmation represents a clear sense of the possible, one that persists despite the overwhelming pain of loss and the temporary failures of love and faith. While Conroy's novels almost always end with the sense that their protagonists have escaped their most persistent demons and that they may begin to heal their emotional wounds, *South of Broad*'s conclusion is arguably his most sanguine. The ambivalence that marks Ben Meecham's appropriation of his father's role in *The Great Santini*, for instance, or Tom Wingo's longing glance toward the bridge that would lead him to Lowenstein in *The Prince of Tides* are not apparent here. Instead the novel's final scene is devoted to a gathering of the remaining members of the original group of friends, and as they look at the Cooper River, they spot a single porpoise break from its school. Trevor utters the word "Sheba" and then immediately apologizes for being "carried away by a rare moment of piffle and nostalgia and even, God forbid, religious sentimentality at its most grotesque" (511). But in a book that exposes its readers to the full horror of the grotesque, there is a disingenuousness to Trevor's apology. Indeed as the group faces east—another echo of *Ulysses,* in which the east is depicted as a space of possibility—Leo is happy to celebrate nostalgia and faith, the bedrocks of Charlestonian life, and simultaneously to imagine a world where "anything can happen" (512).

CODA

The Death of Santini

In his most recent memoir, *The Death of Santini* (2013), Pat Conroy writes that he is fascinated by "the immense and mysterious powers I associate with the perfect shape of a circle" (147), and the memoir seems to delight in its own dizzying spirals as it explores the relationship between Conroy's life and art. *The Death of Santini* revisits a number of episodes familiar to readers of his novels, this time as autobiographical fact, and there are moments when Conroy's lived experiences and fictional work seem to exist in perfect symmetry, confirming his self-identification as the "recording angel" of his family history (2). Yet Conroy also demonstrates that just as his life shapes his fiction, his novels equally impact his life: in *The Death of Santini*, he invites readers to consider the ways in which his family has been altered by the public exposure his work has invited and by the collective introspection it has demanded. Ultimately, however, the memoir suggests that art does not simply shape life, nor life art, but instead that the two exist in a continuous loop, a claim that is most succinctly captured in *The Death of Santini* in a scene in which Don Conroy cries as he watches Bull Meecham's funeral in the film adaptation of *The Great Santini*, momentarily confusing his own identity with the fictional Santini's.

In its exploration of the ways in which experience and fiction function as an improbable Möbius strip, Conroy has created a memoir that is enormously compelling on a number of levels, and indeed it has garnered some of the most enthusiastic reviews of his career. In its central theme, the book also highlights Conroy's unique position in American letters, in which he is simultaneously a serious author and a true literary celebrity. Many readers have gravitated to the book in part because they want to know "the real story" behind his work. (We see this curiosity illustrated in the memoir itself: Conroy recalls that, at her request, he read *The Lords of Discipline* aloud to Peggy Conroy in the final phases of her battle with leukemia, and she would interrupt him to ask, "Did that really happen?" acting as a surrogate for Conroy's larger readership [180].) Yet readers who are drawn to *The Death of Santini* because they want to know more about Conroy as a person are also immersed in his identity as an artist. As Frank Bruni wrote in his review of the memoir, to read the book is to be reminded "of the decadent pleasures of [Conroy's] language, . . . his promiscuous gift for metaphor, and . . . his ability, in the finest passages of his fiction, to make the love, hurt, or terror a protagonist feels seem to be the only emotion the world could possibly have room for, the rightful center of the trembling universe."[1]

Interestingly, though, while *The Death of Santini* is a testament to Conroy's immense popularity and artistic achievement, with this memoir he also proposes to dynamite the rails that have led to his success. He opens the book with the acknowledgment that "I've been writing the story of my own life for over forty years" (1) but then goes to on to identify the memoir specifically as a project that will "examine the wreckage one last time" (12). In explaining that *The Death of Santini* is "a final circling of the block" (12), he suggests that he is moving on to other themes beyond those grounded in his own experience and, accordingly, that *The Death of Santini* is his final backward glance. It is an enormously bold act—unthinkable perhaps—to begin a new chapter so deep into a career that has been focused primarily on a single "obsession" (1). Yet ultimately it also seems in keeping with Conroy's understanding of himself as an author. In his essay "Why I Write" he likens himself to a tightrope walker and says that "I invited readers who chose to make the journey with me to join me on the high wire. I would work without a net and without the noise of the crowd to disturb me."[2] In bidding his parents' legacy adieu in *The Death of Santini*, Conroy climbs on to the high wire again, proposing to take new risks with his art.

NOTES

Chapter 1—Understanding Pat Conroy

1. Conroy, "A Love Letter to Thomas Wolfe," in *My Reading Life*, 241.
2. Simon, "Conroy's *Reading Life*."
3. Powell, "Pat Conroy," 46.
4. Conroy, "Why I Write," in *My Reading Life*, 301.
5. I have not discussed *My Reading Life*, Conroy's collection of essays on reading and writing, holistically in this study but rather draw from it in my discussion of Conroy's major works.
6. Conroy, *Death of Santini*, 1.
7. Berendt, "Conroy Saga," 110.
8. There were also six miscarriages, a remarkable fact in that it means that Peggy Conroy was pregnant or had small children for most of her marriage to Don.
9. Conroy, "Stories," in *Why I Write*, 52; Conroy, introduction to *Military Brats*, xix.
10. Conroy, introduction to *Military Brats*, xviii.
11. Conroy alternately refers to his mother as Peg and Peggy. I have used *Peggy* throughout this study for consistency. Significantly this nickname was given to her in honor of Margaret Mitchell.
12. Conroy, "The Lily," in *My Reading Life*, 15.
13. Rennert, "Family Secrets," 149.
14. According to Conroy, Peggy viewed *Gone with the Wind* as "an anthem of defiance. If you could not defeat the Yankees on the battlefield, then by God, one of your women could rise from the ashes of humiliation to write more powerfully than the enemy and all the historians and novelists who sang the praises of the Union." Conroy, *"Gone with the Wind,"* in *My Reading Life*, 17.
15. Conroy, introduction to *Military Brats*, xix.
16. Conroy sometimes refers to his sister as Carol and at other times Carol Ann, her childhood name. In this study I have used "Carol," the name by which she is known professionally.
17. Powell, "Pat Conroy," 52.
18. Conroy, *Death of Santini*, 70.
19. Conroy has reported that all of his siblings have struggled with depression, stating, "Of the seven of us, five have been suicidal at one time or another. The other two just don't admit it." Tom Conroy succeeded in his suicide attempt, dying in 1994. Minzesheimer, "Pat Conroy Returns."
20. Conroy, *Death of Santini*, March 5, 2013 manuscript, 89.
21. Conroy, *Death of Santini*, 84.

22. Ford, "Pat Conroy's Lowcountry," 85.

23. Conroy has four daughters: Jessica and Melissa, whom he adopted during his marriage to Barbara Bolling Jones; Megan, with Barbara; and, with Lenore Fleischer, Susannah, who severed ties with Conroy after his divorce from her mother. He also served as an active step-parent to Emily Fleischer during his marriage to Lenore and recognizes her as a daughter in the acknowledgments to *My Reading Life.* Fleischer also has one son, Gregory, who was a teenager when she married Conroy.

24. Out of respect for her expressed desire for anonymity, Conroy has written relatively little about his marriage to Barbara Bolling Jones, although he published an essay in 1978, "Anatomy of a Divorce," that recounts the immense pain he suffered during and after their breakup. He has avoided writing about the details of his marriage to Fleischer as well, but has written more generally about the difficult nature of the relationship, often in unforgiving terms. In *My Losing Season,* for example, he writes, "If Lenore had been a country, I would have married North Korea, this is how murderous, cut off, and isolated the marriage had begun to seem to me" (11).

25. Berendt, "Conroy Saga," 110.

26. Rennert, "Family Secrets," 81.

27. Conroy, *My Reading Life,* 335. Conroy and King were recently deemed "the South's most notable literary couple" by *Garden and Gun,* an upscale southern lifestyle magazine ("Back Porch Session: Pat Conroy and Cassandra King," *Garden and Gun,* October 2013, http://gardenandgun.com/media/back-porch-session-pat-conroy-and-cassandra-king). See also Dam, "Pat Conroy," and Arnold, "Making Books."

28. Conroy, *Death of Santini,* March 5, 2013, manuscript, 418.

29. Aherns, "Waves of Memory."

30. Conroy, *My Losing Season,* 292. Conroy has also spoken of readers who erroneously conflate his novels' autobiographical origins with his actual lived experiences. He notes that fans will "say things like, 'It was awful what happened to your brother Luke' [a character in *The Prince of Tides*]. I'll say, 'I don't have a brother Luke.' They argue with me about this brother Luke. I've had people meet my father and gasp. They'll say, 'But you're dead. I read it in *The Great Santini.* I saw the movie. I saw the burial.' They identify so strongly that the aspects of fictionalizing get lost in the confusion when I said I write autobiographically." Walsh, "Interview," 201.

31. Conroy has said, "I used alcohol the way other people use Prozac. . . . It was my drug of choice." Castro, "Sober and Confident," 59.

32. See, review of *My Reading Life.*

33. "Eulogy for Doug Marlette," PatConroy.com, July 14, 2007. http://www.patconroy .com/articles_eulogy-dm.php.

34. Conroy, personal interview, March 7, 2013.

35. Weaver, "Interview."

36. Conroy, *Death of Santini,* 64; Walsh, "Interview," 201.

37. Walsh, "Interview," 217–18.

38. Conroy, "Love Letter to Thomas Wolfe," 243.

39. Conroy, "Southerner in Paris," in *My Reading Life,* 215, 235.

40. Conroy, "Why I Write," 304.

41. Conroy has said that he initially set this goal for himself "because I knew that I would come to the writing of books without the weight of culture and learning that a well-established, confidently placed family could offer its children." He continues to devote himself to the study of language: his journals are filled with long lists of words

that he has encountered in his reading and that appeal to him because of their sound or nuance. Conroy, "Why I Write," 310.

42. Conroy, "Love Letter to Thomas Wolfe," 239–40, 239.

43. Ibid., 247.

44. Conroy, foreword to *Magical Campus*, xi.

45. William Faulkner, *Absalom, Absalom!* (New York: Vintage, 1986), 142; Michael Kreyling, *Inventing Southern Literature* (Jackson: University Press of Mississippi), xiv.

46. Conroy, "Love Letter to Thomas Wolfe," 264.

47. Comparisons between Wolfe's style and themes and Conroy's are found throughout criticism of Conroy's work. See, in particular, Idol, "(Un)Blest Be the Ties." Connections are also often made between the relationship of Wolfe and his editor, Maxwell Perkins, and that of Conroy and Nan Talese; both editors are recognized as working with the authors to shape often massive first drafts of works. See, for instance, Blades, "Writer's Best Friend."

48. Conroy, "Love Letter to Thomas Wolfe," 243–44.

49. Conroy, "*Gone with the Wind*," 31.

50. Conroy, *Death of Santini*, 46.

51. Conroy, "Why I Write," 303; Conroy, *Death of Santini*, 47.

52. The introductions and prefaces Conroy has written reflect his varied interests and connections. In addition to writing introductions for a number of canonical works, Thomas Wolfe's *Of Time and the River* and Leo Tolstoy's *War and Peace* among them, he has also written introductions to cookbooks, including those written by celebrated chef Frank Stitt, Conroy's former Daufuskie student Sallie Ann Robinson, and novelist Janis Owens; art folios, including collections of work by photographer Jack Leigh and Gullah painter Jonathan Green; and collected essays, including those devoted to the work of Wolfe and James Dickey.

53. Conroy, personal interview, March 7, 2013.

54. Parker, "Writing Life." Conroy envisions this project as a response to the work of influential auteurs, but his prior connection to film has taken many forms. He was nominated for an Oscar in 1992 for his work on the screenplay of *The Prince of Tides,* and he has flirted with a number of other film projects, including a screenplay written with Doug Marlette, *Ex,* and a proposed adaptation of Wolfe's *Look Homeward, Angel.*

55. Conroy, personal interview, November 16, 2013.

Chapter 2—*The Water Is Wide*

1. Conroy, introduction to *The Boo*, n.p. The book is, indeed, generally identified as an amateur effort. In his book *Pat Conroy: A Critical Companion,* for instance, Landon C. Burns identifies *The Boo* as "a not-very-good book" (29).

2. Conroy, introduction to *The Boo*, n.p.

3. Fred Hobson, *But Now I See: The White Southern Racial Conversion Narrative* (Baton Rouge: Louisiana State University Press, 1999).

4. Interestingly when the schoolhouse is no longer needed for George Stone, it is turned into a residence for Mrs. Brown. She thus literally inhabits the legacy of Jim Crow.

5. This symbolism is made richer by the fact that the overwhelming majority of Yamacrawans cannot swim. To try to enter the water is to risk literal, and metaphorical, drowning.

6. The students cannot pronounce *Conroy* and call him "Conrack" instead, thus rechristening him as one of their own.

7. The threat of Vietnam was quite real to Conroy, who was drafted shortly after he was fired from his position on Daufuskie. For a full account, see Conroy, *Death of Santini*, 43–45.

8. Conroy also sees this impulse reflected in the work of the "California boys," a rotating series of college students who come to the island to do good works and often find themselves assigned to building latrines, "putting their burning liberalism to the test of the sword" (110).

9. While Conroy is quick to identify the paradoxes that underlie his liberal impulses, the memoir is marked by more oblique references to racial anxiety as well. For instance he remarks on his fear of the dark at several points in *The Water Is Wide*, and darkness is further aligned with blackness when one "coal black night" the "face of a grinning black man" appears just outside his window, filling Conroy with "fright and shock" (84). Conroy later determines the man is Mad Billie, an innocuous figure who exploits his "madness" to earn a living doing odd jobs on the island: yet in his initial appearance, Mad Billie represents the terror implicit in forms of the "racial other."

10. Conroy, *Death of Santini*, 42.

11. Conroy, undated journal, uncollected papers.

12. Conroy, "My Teacher, James Dickey," in *My Reading Life*, 296. Dickey later wrote to Conroy, "There is no student of mine of whom I am more proud. . . . You and I are both creatures of the Word. We want *this* word, rather than this word's second cousin twice removed. And that exclusiveness will save us, I do believe." James Dickey, letter to Pat Conroy, March 1, 1999, uncollected papers.

13. Conroy, *Death of Santini*, 45–46.

14. Ibid., 46.

15. Conroy, "Julian Bach," in *Pat Conroy Cookbook*, 268. Gary Abrams has noted that this story "has achieved the status of a staple anecdote" (Abrams, "Novelist"). In a related story, Conroy further revealed himself to be an innocent in the publishing world when Bach called him to tell him the good news that *The Water Is Wide* had been accepted by Houghton Mifflin for $7,500. Conroy, who had self-published *The Boo*, says he told Bach, "But, Julian, I can get it done a lot cheaper down here," not understanding that the $7,500 was to be his payment, not the cost he would bear to release the book. Conroy, "Julian Bach," 271.

16. After the publication of *The Water Is Wide*, the National Education Association granted Conroy its Humanitarian Award, and throughout his career he has continued to be an advocate for teachers.

17. Conroy, *Death of Santini*, 48. Conroy returned to nearby Fripp Island in 1989 and then moved back to the town of Beaufort proper in 2011.

18. Broyard, "Supererogating Down South"; Haskins, "Rural Education." Along these lines James J. Buckley Jr.'s review in *America* focused on Conroy's "realization that he should have tried to fight this system by working through it" and sees the book as demonstrating that "a teacher may acquire the wings to fly over educational adversities, when the water is wide." Buckley, review of *The Water Is Wide*, 181.

19. Interestingly Kael notes that "reading the book after seeing the movie, I discovered (once again) that everything that bothered me in the movie was the result of a cut or an addition." Pauline Kael, "A Brash Young Man," *New Yorker*, March 11, 1974, 120–21.

20. Eugenia Collier, "Once Again, the White Liberal to the Rescue," review of *Conrack*, dir. Martin Ritt, *New York Times*, April 21, 1974.

21. Karimi, "Water Is Wide," 259.

22. Ibid. Conroy has always been measured in his enthusiasm about *Conrack,* identifying it at one point as "syrupy." See Carlton Jackson, *Picking Up the Tab: The Life and Movies of Martin Ritt* (Bowling Green, Ohio: Bowling Green University Press, 1994), 134.

Chapter 3—*The Great Santini*

1. Conroy, *Death of Santini,* 53. Conroy began the project as a work of autobiography but "had to pull back from that outraged narrative voice" because he found it to be "too venomous and unforgiving." Moreover he has said he had to fictionalize—and soften—his childhood because his editor feared that accounts of the domestic abuse that Conroy, his siblings, and his mother suffered at the hands of his father would not be believed by readers. He writes, "To make my father human, I had to lie." Conroy, *Death of Santini,* 53, 54.

2. The Freudian framework of the novel is often remarked on by critics, but it is highlighted by Conroy as well. In their first exchange in the novel, Mary Anne playfully calls Ben "Oedipus" after he remarks on Lillian's beauty (18).

3. Lillian's sentimentalizing of Toomer as "all the South used to be and all it should still be" raises a number of issues, and just as Lillian's relationship with Arrabelle is shaded by the paradoxes and complexities of race in the early 1960s, Ben's friendship with Toomer exists within the context of a social and cultural history of which he is often unaware, even as he is shaped by it (439). For example, when he first meets Toomer, we are told that, "Ben had never studied the features of the black man who was simply a part of the landscape, of no more interest to him than a storefront or a balustrade. Now, with the addition of Arrabelle to the household, the flower boy had a name, Toomer Smalls. As the wagon neared the house, he began to have a face" (107–8). Not only is Ben initially complicit in Toomer's relative invisibility in Ravenel, then, but the shifting use of "boy" and "man" in this passage speaks to the power of race to undermine masculinity, a dynamic that is particularly of note in a text preoccupied with defining manhood.

4. In a lovely inversion of this truth, Conroy writes that Don Conroy "delivered me the last chapters" of *The Great Santini* by enacting a crash scene for Pat, pretending to be a pilot in the doomed plane as Pat watched and took notes. Conroy, "A Recipe Is a Story," in *Pat Conroy Cookbook,* 102.

5. William Faulkner, *Absalom, Absalom!* (1936; New York: Random House, 2011), 303. Quentin is replying to a question put to him by his Harvard roommate, Shreve: "Why do you hate the South?"

6. In a perfect blurring of life and art, Conroy has written about the behavior of his sister Carol, at the funeral of their brother Tom in 1994, almost twenty years after the publication of *The Great Santini.* Just as Mary Anne, who was modeled after Carol, flings her tears in *The Great Santini,* Carol creates a "ball of tears" out of the tissues she has used over two days, tossing and catching it throughout the funeral service as a visual articulation of her grief and anger. Conroy, *Death of Santini,* 229.

7. Ben and Mary Anne's younger sister, Karen, is often overlooked as well, and in a scene that functions in parallel to Mary Anne's awkward and hyper-sexualized confrontation of her father, Karen earnestly tries to tell Ben that she's gotten her period and is "a woman now" (353). Ben, uncomfortable with any mention of sexuality after years of strict Catholic schooling, asks Karen about her grades in response, in effect echoing Bull's dismissal of Mary Anne.

8. Conroy, *Death of Santini,* 66.

9. Conroy told a reporter that after overdosing on pills, "I woke up. I was very surprised" (Castro, "Sober and Confident," 58). He ultimately sought help from Dr. Marion O'Neill, the therapist whom he has credited with saving his life during this period and who worked with him again during later depressive episodes.

10. Conroy, *Death of Santini*, 72.

11. Ibid., 73.

12. Ibid., 74–75.

13. Ibid., 40.

14. Ibid., 113. The film version of *The Great Santini* was a commercial and critical success and is now viewed as something of a classic. Interestingly the movie was initially deemed a failure and risked being buried. For a brief overview of the film's commercial history, see Tom Buckley, "'Great Santini' Teaches Doubters a Lesson," *New York Times,* July 21, 1980.

Chapter 4—*The Lords of Discipline*

1. Conroy, introduction to *The Boo,* n.p.

2. Conroy, introduction to *The Boo,* n.p.; Conroy, *Death of Santini,* 103.

3. Interestingly Conroy had originally intended Ben Meecham to be the protagonist of *The Lords of Discipline.* He had long believed that Thomas Wolfe's work lost some of its potency when Wolfe abandoned Eugene Gant as his protagonist, and thus Conroy envisioned his own oeuvre as following a single doppelgänger through the signal events of his life. After he had made significant progress on the manuscript of *The Lords of Discipline,* however, he learned that the rights to the character of Ben Meecham had been sold along with *The Great Santini,* and thus he had to rewrite *The Lords of Discipline* with a new character at its center, giving him a unique history and sensibility. Conroy, personal interview, November 16, 2013.

4. In a glossary he wrote for *The Boo,* Conroy lists the term *knob* as synonymous with "plebe, dumbhead, screw, wad, waste, nut, abortion, [and] fourth-classman," all terms that are used to signify a freshman (172).

5. Trent Watts, "Telling White Men's Stories," in *White Masculinity in the Recent South,* edited by Trent Watts (Baton Rouge: Louisiana State University Press, 2000), 2.

6. Bertram Wyatt-Brown, *Southern Honor: Ethics and Behavior in the Old South* (Oxford: Oxford University Press, 1982), 114, 4.

7. Burns, *Pat Conroy,* 81.

8. Conroy notes that "most cadets loved the book. . . . When I went for an autographing, there were Citadel people just lined up," suggesting that disapproval of the book reflected an institutional perspective rather than a personal one. William Walsh, "Interview," 206.

9. Conroy not only was a vocal supporter of Faulkner in her quest for admission, but he also continued to pay her tuition at Anderson College in South Carolina after she was driven out of the Citadel during Hell Week. Speaking about his support of Faulkner, he has said, "I wanted a Citadel man to pay for Shannon's college education. That was important to me." See Bob Meadows, "Fresh Start," *People Magazine,* June 28, 2004, 146.

10. Rose, "Martial Spirit." Similarly Margaret Manning raved about the novel in her review for the *Boston Globe,* praising "the flavor, vitality, humor, and of course the seriousness, the sadness of this remarkable novel" (Manning, "Hazy Days"). In another example of this type of response, in a capsule review in the *Saturday Review,* Julia Stone Peters expressed skepticism of the novel's "seriousness" but also wrote that "*The Lords*

of Discipline is engrossing and well-written" and praised in particular Conroy's "funny, fluent prose" (Peters, review of *The Lords of Discipline*, 87).

11. Crews, "Passage to Manhood." Writing in *Southern Cultures* in 2010, Steve Estes echoed Crews's complaint, positing that "*Lords of Discipline* has all of the subtlety of a 1950's melodrama or a steamy romance novel (befitting the airbrushed cover of the paperback)," a point that also raises issues about the early marketing of Conroy's work and the role it may have played in his acceptance in the canon. Estes, "Long, Gay Line," 48.

Chapter 5—*The Prince of Tides*

1. Conroy has worked with a number of esteemed editors: Shannon Ravenel, now director of her own imprint at Algonquin Books, edited *The Water Is Wide*; Anne Barrett edited *The Great Santini;* and Jonathan Galassi, now president and publisher of Farrar, Straus and Giroux, edited *The Lords of Discipline.*

2. Qtd. in Ferguson, "Writer and His Refuge." Conroy completed *The Lords of Discipline* while in Paris, and he has written, "I've always thought that writers should spend part of their lives testing themselves in the crucibles of alien cultures." Conroy, "Letter from Rome," in *Pat Conroy Cookbook,* 133.

3. Jonathan Galassi, letter to Pat Conroy, May 28, 1986, uncollected papers.

4. Tom learns to cook when Sallie is in medical school, and it is interesting that food does not become a marker of his emasculation but rather contains displaced desire; throughout the novel meals are described in erotic language and function as the site of uninhibited pleasure for Tom.

5. Significantly Savannah's work is often quoted at length in the novel, allowing her to be heard even when she has succumbed to the silence of psychosis. In fact the title of the novel, a reference to Luke, is taken from her work.

6. To a lesser extent, Tom also probes racial boundaries, as is evinced in his support of Benji Washington, the first black student to attend Colleton High School. The novel's treatment of race is more limited than in *The Great Santini* or *The Lords of Discipline,* however, and while Tom does find satisfaction in recognizing Benji as a social equal— and his athletic superior—the episodes involving Benji are as interested in the transformative power of sport as they are an extended consideration of southern racism.

7. Judaism is also depicted as essentially othering its southern adherents in the novel. As Lowenstein points out when Tom complains of feeling his Catholicism has alienated him in the South, "You have no idea who weird it is to be raised Jewish anywhere in the world (62)." Yet, she also fiercely holds on to her identity as a Jew, keeping her maiden name after her marriage to Herbert Woodruff, a gentile. Conroy would go on to explore Jewish identity in more depth in *Beach Music.*

8. Indeed Henry's power dissipates after his children are grown, and he is almost entirely absent from the narrative after his divorce when he is jailed after a botched attempt at drug running, his most ill-advised entrepreneurial project.

9. In a convincingly-argued essay, critic P. Ellen Malphrus has arged that Luke's death solidifies his role as a hero in the model codified by Jospeh Campbell. Such a depiction of Luke doesn't fully acknowledge the novel's skepticism of martyrdom, however. Both Sarah Jenkins, the nursemaid who helps to save the children shortly after the twins are born, and Gunter Kraus, the priest who saves Henry, die as a result of their service. Tom notes, "Later, I would wonder if their courage and sacrifice, the selfless, mortal choices that led to their own ruin and to the survival of the house of Wingo was no part of some obscene joke whose punch line would take years to evolve (98)." Certainly, Tom

is critical of the Wingos' relative value here, but he also suggests that the causes that seem to merit martyrdom often cannot sustain their promise. See P. Ellen Malphrus, "*The Prince of Tides* as Archeypal Hero Quest."

10. See James Hibberd, "Conroy's *Tides* Rolling into ABC," *Hollywood Reporter,* September 16, 2010.

11. Bass, "Prince of Pain"; Kilpatrick, review of *The Prince of Tides,* 108.

12. Godwin, "Romancing the Shrink." This view is echoed in reviews such as Rhoda Koenig's in *New York,* which identified the novel's "nice small moments" as "drowned in the flood of Mighty Wurlitzer music" (Koenig, review of *The Prince of Tides,* 136). Many reviews are also more balanced, such as Brigitte Weeks's assessment in the *Washington Post Book World* that the "novel is monstrously long, yet a pleasure to read, flawed yet stuffed to the end papers with lyricism, melodrama, anguish, and plain old suspense. Given all that, one can brush aside its lapses like troublesome flies" (Weeks, "Pat Conroy").

13. Willistein, "Southern Way."

14. Powell, "Pat Conroy," 49; Walsh, "Interview" 207–8, 202.

15. *The Prince of Tides* was also engaged in a more public controversy when a fundamentalist minister in Charleston, West Virginia, called for the removal of the novel from an eleventh-grade advanced placement reading list. (*Beach Music* was later the subject of similar controversy.) For a succinct summary of the debate, see White, "Pat Conroy's 'Gutter Language.'"

16. After Carol withdrew her work, Conroy was compelled to write poems in Savannah's voice on short notice, a task that he has said "scared me very badly." Walsh, "Interview," 217.

17. Conroy, *Death of Santini,* March 5, 2013, manuscript, 90.

18. Rennert, "Family Secrets," 80. Conroy has said that she knew the book contained a fuller portrait of her, asking Conroy at one point, "This time it's me, isn't it?" and, in a wonderfully illustrative move, later telling him, "I'd like Meryl Streep to play the role." Rennert, "Family Secrets," 80; Conroy, *Death of Santini,* 175.

19. Don Conroy's aggressive denials of his behavior reached their apex in 1991 when he was featured in an article in *Atlanta Magazine.* In the story he mocked his reputation and suggested that "Pat can be so convincing and so committed he's persuaded himself this stuff happened." Coppola, "Great Santini Talks Back," 58.

Chapter 6—*Beach Music*

1. For a concise account of the controversy, see Richard Shumate, "Life after Kovach," *Washington Journalism Review* 14, no. 7 (1992): 28–32.

2. Conroy, *Death of Santini,* 261.

3. Ibid.

4. Conroy, *Death of Santini,* early manuscript, 339, uncollected papers.

5. For a discussion of the financial aspects of the book's publication, see Daisy Maryles, "The Conroy Sales Wave," *Publishers Weekly,* July 10, 1995, 16, and Nathan Paul, "Heavy Bidding," *Publishers Weekly,* May 23, 1994, 46. Incidentally, like Conroy's previous novels, *Beach Music* was optioned as a film, but it has been shelved for several years because of legal wrangling within the production company that owns the rights. In his profile of Conroy for *Vanity Fair,* John Berendt suggests that he was "beginning to run out of money" before the publication of *Beach Music.* Berendt, "Conroy Saga," 139.

6. Powell, "Pat Conroy," 55.

7. Conroy, *My Losing Season,* 12.

8. Conroy, *Death of Santini*, 259.

9. As Conroy's "Note to the Reader" suggests, *Beach Music* was the result of exhaustive research, and its plot was inspired in part by a pamphlet describing the experiences of the Stanislawow Jews during the Holocaust that had been translated by the father of a longtime friend of Conroy's, Old New York Bookshop owner Cliff Graubart.

10. Indeed the first draft of *Beach Music* that Conroy submitted to Talese was considerably longer, coming in at 2,100 manuscript pages. See Berendt, "Conroy Saga," 140.

11. Even the most glowing of *Beach Music*'s reviews tended to identify the novel as at least slightly overburdened. Writing in the *San Francisco Review of Books,* for example, Don Paul recognized the novel as "erratic, flawed, and magnificent" (Paul, review of *Beach Music*), and the *Washington Post*'s Brigitte Weeks, who identified Conroy as an "astonishing novelist," said the book is "a chaotic, often exasperating, but completely loveable novel" (Weeks, "Where Stories Sizzle"). Similarly Michael Harris's review in the *Los Angeles Times* argued that "largeness suits Conroy, just as minimalism has suited Raymond Carver and Anne Beattie. *Beach Music* is blockbuster writing at its best" (Harris, "Bigger Than Ever").

Other reviewers were more pointed in their evaluations. R. Z. Sheppard objected to the novel's broad scope in a review in *Time,* arguing, "The historical carpetbagging doesn't add much of anything to the novel except a few unnecessarily grisly shocks" (Sheppard, "First-Person Portentous"), and in his review for the *New York Times,* Christopher Lehmann-Haupt argued that Conroy's ambitions give the work an unexpectedly imitative feel: "In the story of Jack's mother's upbringing, Mr. Conroy tries to out-Faulkner *Sanctuary*. In a tale about how Jack and his friends harpooned a gigantic manta ray, he tries to out-Hemingway *The Old Man and the Sea*. And in the Foxes' horrifying accounts of their Holocaust experiences, he tries to out-Styron *Sophie's Choice*" (Lehmann-Haupt, "Lure of Entanglements").

What is most remarkable about many of these reviews, however, is the new savagery of their tone. Laura Shapiro began her capsule review in *Newsweek,* for example, by asking, "How bad is Pat Conroy's new novel? Let's count the ways" (Shapiro, review of *Beach Music*), Writing in the *New York Times,* Tom Shone claimed, "Jack McCall has got to be the most monstrously smug creation since Robert Kincaid in *The Bridges of Madison County*" (Shone, "You Can Go Home Again"), and Mark Harris wrote in *Entertainment Weekly* that *Beach Music* is "an exploded piñata of a novel that spills its contents across your lap, hoping you'll find something to your taste" (Harris, "Southern Discomfort"). Interestingly the vast majority of reviewers, even those who were most critical of the novel, praised Conroy when he is working on more familiar ground. Harris, for example, wrote that "when Conroy keeps his scale small, the book's sloppy emotionalism can give way to shapely sentimentality," and Sheppard noted, "when Conroy writes about the pleasures of eating boiled crab on tables covered with yesterday's newspaper, when he celebrates the lowcountry's amphibious charms or confronts his mixed feelings about bubba culture, there are flashes of a gifted novelist."

12. Indeed in an oft-quoted line from Conroy's address to the American Booksellers Association in 1985, he amusingly defined the gothic in contemporary southern literature: "My mother, southern to the bone, once told me, 'All southern literature can be summed up in these words: 'On the night the hogs ate Willie, Mama died when she heard what Daddy did to Sister.'"

13. It is interesting that Lucy's story is narrated in the third person. Both of the Foxes' stories are told in the first person and thus have the feel of personal revelation;

Max Rusoff's story, conversely, is told in the third person, reinforcing its identification as an oft-recounted tale that can be legitimately narrated by its former listeners. There is thus a suggestion that Jack has considered his mother's story enough times that it has become familiar to him and that he is comfortable relaying it.

This sort of claim becomes more viable given the extensive thought Conroy gave the narrative voice in the novel. He has explained in interviews that he originally wrote *Beach Music* in the third person at Nan Talese's urging, because she feared that "the first-person with me would always sound like Tom Wingo." After reading a completed draft of the manuscript, however, she reversed her judgment, and Conroy rewrote the novel in the first person. Powell, "Pat Conroy," 54.

14. Capers later also betrays Ledare when he marries her and then leaves her for a younger woman.

Chapter 7—*My Losing Season*

1. Freiert, review of *My Losing Season*, 51. See also Hamblin, "Sports Imagery."

2. Personal interview, March 7, 2013.

3. See Jones, "Conroy's Literary Slam-Dunk"; Howard, "Word-Stung in Beaufort," 64. See also Miles, "Winning Isn't Everything," and Lyons, "Conroy's Losses Add Up to a Win."

4. David, "Ecstasy of Defeat."

5. Creamer, "Hoop Dreams."

6. It is worth noting that unlike other college basketball players, the Citadel Bulldogs have already been beaten down in the barracks, a fact that Thompson chooses to ignore.

7. Miles, "Winning Isn't Everything."

8. Interestingly, as Conroy develops a clearer sense of himself, he also struggles with a faltering faith. He touches on the subject only glancingly in the memoir, writing, "I was receiving the Eucharist every day of my life and fighting [a] war with faithlessness with every cell of my body, but I could feel the withdrawal taking place without my consent" (275). Significantly, writing, which serves as an imaginative act of communion with his father, also helps Conroy to address this gap of faith; writing from his present-day perspective, Conroy notes that he writes because "it's the form that praying takes in me" (303).

9. *My Losing Season* also has moments of overlap with *The Death of Santini*, a book it both predates and predicts: in one scene, for example, Conroy tells his father that he will write about him in a memoir titled *The Death of Santini*, to which Don, who is suffering from colon cancer, remarks, "Hey, great title. You know how to make a guy feel swell" (390).

10. Conroy told a reporter that he treated *My Losing Season* as a work of journalism, explaining, "I'd go to each house and, like you are doing now, I'd interview [my teammates]. I'd have cross-references. Danny Moore [*sic*] would say this happened, 'Do you remember it that way?' And they would say, 'No, there's one thing he got wrong: I didn't say that, I said this.' 'Johnny said you said this.'" Even with this exhaustive process, Conroy accepts that "all of us know that every word can't be true. [But] there is the truth in there." Parker, "Q&A."

11. Turrentine, "When Life Was a Battle."

12. Jordan tells his father, "America's a good enough country to die for even when America's wrong. At least, for a boy like me. Raised the way you and Mom raised me" (714).

13. Sandomir, "Recipes for a Novelist's Memoirs."

14. See John T. Edge, ed., *The New Encyclopedia of South Culture*, vol. 7: *Foodways* (Chapel Hill: University of North Carolina Press, 2007).

15. John Lanchester, "Incredible Edibles: The Mad Genius of 'Modernist Cuisine,'" *New Yorker*, March 21, 2011, 64–68.

Chapter 8—*South of Broad*

1. For a discussion of the ways in which Conroy appropriates and reinterprets Joyce, see Bryan Giemza, *Irish Catholic Writers and the Invention of the American South* (Baton Rouge: Louisiana State University Press, 2013), 241–49.

2. Representative of these complaints is Scott Martelle's observation in the *Los Angeles Times* that "tragic twists just appear, lacking the kind of build-up that makes them work" (Martelle, review of *South of Broad*). Similarly Susan Whithall concluded her review in the *Detroit News* by stating that "the narrative strains credulity" (Whithall, "Pat Conroy").

Almost all reviews praised Conroy's prose. In his review for the *Washington Post,* for example, Chris Bohjalian wrote that despite his marked criticisms of the book, "I still turned the pages with relish. Conroy is an immensely gifted stylist, and there are passage in the novel that are lush and beautiful and precise" (Bohjalian, "Prince of Tears"). Similarly Roy Hoffman wrote in the *New York Times* that "Conroy remains a magician of the page. As a writer, he owns the South Carolina coast" (Hoffman, "Reunited").

In an interview published in the paperback edition of the novel, Conroy seems to have anticipated reviewers' accusations of implausibility, and he notes that, as is true of almost all of his work, his characters and situations are often borrowed from reality, identifying the real-life inspiration for many of *South of Broad's* seemingly more fantastic plot points.

3. Minzesheimer, "Pat Conroy Returns."

4. Conroy, *Death of Santini*, 70.

5. Conroy's inclusion of Caen, whom he came to know when he was living in San Francisco after the publication of *The Prince of Tides,* is a nod to Joyce's incorporation of real people and places in *Ulysses*.

6. In another nod to Joyce, Molly recalls *Ulysses*'s Molly Bloom, Leopold's wayward wife.

Coda—*The Death of Santini*

1. Bruni, "Running Battles."

2. Conroy, "Why I Write," 301.

BIBLIOGRAPHY

Primary Works

BOOKS BY CONROY

The Boo. 1970. Atlanta: Old New York Book Shop Press, 2005.
The Water Is Wide. 1972. New York: Dial, 2009.
The Great Santini. 1976. New York: Dial, 2006.
The Lords of Discipline. 1980. New York: Dial, 2006.
The Prince of Tides. 1986. New York: Dial, 2009.
Beach Music. 1995. New York: Dial, 2009.
My Losing Season. New York, Doubleday, 2002.
The Pat Conroy Cookbook: Recipes and Stories of My Life, with Susanne Williamson
    Pollack. New York: Doubleday, 2004.
South of Broad. 2009. New York: Dial, 2010.
My Reading Life. New York: Doubleday, 2010.
The Death of Santini. New York, Doubleday, 2013.

SELECTED ESSAYS AND INTRODUCTIONS BY CONROY

"Anatomy of a Divorce." *Atlanta Magazine,* November 1978, 43.
Foreword to *The Magical Campus: The North Carolina Writings,* by Thomas Wolfe.
    Ed. Matthew J. Bruccoli and Aldo P. Magi. Columbia: University of South Carolina
    Press, 2008, xi–xiv.
Introduction to *Military Brats: Legacies of Childhood inside the Fortress,* by Mary
    Edwards Wertsch. New York: Harmony Books, 1991, xvii–xxv.
"Stories." In *Why I Write: Thoughts on the Craft of Fiction,* edited by Will Blythe,
    47–60. New York: Little, Brown, 2005.

INTERVIEWS

Howard, Hugh. "Word-Stung in Beaufort: Pat Conroy." In *Writers of the American
    South: Their Literary Landscapes,* 53–69. New York: Rizzoli, 2005.
Karimi, A. M. "The Water Is Wide: A Interview with Pat Conroy." *New Orleans Review*
    4, no. 3 (1974): 257–59.
Parker, Adam. "Q&A with Pat Conroy and Cassandra King." *Charleston Post and
    Courier,* September 22, 2013.
Powell, Dannye Romine. "Pat Conroy." In *Parting the Curtains: Interviews with South-
    ern Writers,* 46–63. Winston-Salem, N.C.: Blair, 1994.
Rennert, Amy. "Family Secrets." *San Francisco Focus,* December 1991, 77.
Simon, Scott. "Conroy's *Reading Life:* A Search for Safe Harbors." *Weekend Edition,*
    NPR, November 6, 2010.

Walsh, William. "Interview: Pat Conroy." *Other Voices* no. 11 (1989): 200–218.

Weaver, Teresa. "Interview with Pat Conroy." *Atlanta*, September 1, 2009. http://www
.atlantamagazine.com/features/2013/09/30/interview-with-pat-conroy.

Young, Robin. "Interview with Pat Conroy." *Here and Now*, NPR, November 19, 2003.

Selected Works about Pat Conroy

Abrams, Garry. "Novelist Turns Adversity into Profit." *Los Angeles Times*, December
12, 1986.

Aherns, Frank. "Waves of Memory: With *Beach Music*, Author Pat Conroy Swims Back
to the Surface." Review of *Beach Music. Washington Post*, July 21, 1995.

Arnold, Martin. "Making Books: Two Writers under One Roof." *New York Times*,
October 24, 2002.

Bass, Judy. "A Prince of Pain." *Chicago Tribune Books*, October 19, 1986.

Berendt, John. "The Conroy Saga." *Vanity Fair*, July 1995, 108.

Blades, John. "A Writer's Best Friend." *Chicago Tribune*, October 26, 1990.

Bohjalian, Chris. "The Prince of Tears." Review of *South of Broad. Washington Post*,
August 11, 2009.

Broyard, Anatole. "Supererogating Down South." Review of *The Water Is Wide. New
York Times*, July 13, 1972.

Bruni, Frank. "Running Battles." Review of *The Death of Santini. New York Times
Book Review*. Noember 15, 2013: 14.

Buckley, James A., Jr. Review of *The Water Is Wide. America*, September 16, 1972, 181.

Burns, Landon C. *Pat Conroy: A Critical Companion*. Westport, Conn.: Greenwood,
1996.

Castro, Peter. "Sober and Confident." *People Magazine*, August 14, 1995, 55–59.

Cochran, Tracy. "A Winning Career." *Publishers Weekly*, September 30, 2002, 41–43.

Coppola, Vincent. "The Great Santini Talks Back." *Atlanta Magazine*, September 1991,
56.

Creamer, Robert W. "Hoop Dreams." Review of *My Losing Season. Washington Post
Book World*, October 20, 2002.

Crews, Harry. "The Passage to Manhood." Review of *The Lords of Discipline. New
York Times Book Review*, December 7, 1980.

Dam, Julie K. L. "Pat Conroy: Book of Love." *People Magazine*, November 11, 2002,
115–16.

David, Grainger. "Ecstasy of Defeat." Review of *My Losing Season. Fortune*, October
28, 2002, 228.

Estes, Steve. "The Long Gay Line: Gender and Sexual Orientation at The Citadel."
Southern Cultures 16, no. 1 (2010): 46–64.

Ferguson, Stuart. "The Writer and His Refuge." *Wall Street Journal*, August 25, 2009.

Ford, Gary D. "Pat Conroy's Lowcountry." *Southern Living*, September 2004, 5: 82–89.

Freiert, William. Review of *The Prince of Tides. Classical Myth and Modern Literature
Quarterly* 10 (1989): 51.

Godwin, Gail. "Romancing the Shrink." Review of *The Prince of Tides. New York
Times Book Review*, October 12, 1986.

Gorner, Peter, "An Author 'Blessed' by Unhappiness." *Chicago Tribune*, November 25,
1986.

Hamblin, Robert. "Sports Imagery in Pat Conroy's Novels." *Aethlon* 10, no. 1 (1993):
49–59.

Harris, Mark. "Southern Discomfort." Review of *Beach Music*. *Entertainment Weekly*, June 30, 1995 92.

Harris, Michael, "Bigger Than Ever." Review of *Beach Music*. *Los Angeles Times*, July 25, 1995.

Haskins, Jim. "Rural Education Sea Islands Style." Review of *The Water Is Wide*. *New York Times Book Review*, September 24, 1972.

Hoffman, Roy. "Reunited." Review of *Beach Music*. *New York Times Book Review*, August 20, 2009.

Idol, John. "(Un)Blest Be the Ties That Bind: The Dysfunctional Family in *Look Homeward, Angel* and *The Great Santini*." *North Carolina Literary Review* 9 (2000): 142–50.

Jones, Malcolm. "Conroy's Literary Slam-Dunk." Review of *My Losing Season*. *Newsweek*, October 14, 2002, 63–64.

Kilpatrick, Thomas. Review of *The Prince of Tides*. *Library Journal*, October 15, 1986, 108.

Koenig, Rhoda. Review of *The Prince of Tides*. *New York*, October 27, 1986, 135–36.

Lehmann-Haupt, Christopher. "Lure of Entanglements Home Grown and Lasting." Review of *Beach Music*. *New York Times*, July 24, 1995.

Lyons, Kevin. "Conroy's Losses Add Up to a Win." Review of *My Losing Season*. *Detroit Free Press* November 10, 2002.

Klein, Julia M. "Larger Than Life." *Philadelphia Inquirer*, August 31, 1995. http://articles .philly.com/1995-08-31/living/25710892_1_donald-conroy-don-conroy-pat-conroy.

Malphrus, P. Ellen. "The Prince of Tides as Archetypal Hero Quest." *The Southern Literary Journal* 30, no. 2 (2007): 100–118.

Martelle, Scott. Review of *South of Broad*. *Los Angeles Times*, August 11, 2009. http:// articles.latimes.com/2009/aug/11/entertainment/et-book11.

Manning, Margaret. "Hazy Days in the Good Ol' South." Review of *The Lords of Discipline*. *Boston Globe*, October 5, 1980.

Miles, Jonathan. "Winning Isn't Everything." Review of *My Losing Season*. *New York Times*, October 27, 2002.

Minzesheimer, Bob. "Pat Conroy Returns to Familiar Turf with *South of Broad*." *USA Today*, August 8, 2009.

Parker, Adam. "The Writing Life." *Charleston Post and Courier*, September 22, 2013.

Paul, Don. Review of *Beach Music*. *San Francisco Review of Books* 20:3 (July/Aug. 1995).

Peters, Julia Stone. "Review of *The Lords of Discipline*." *The Saturday Review*. Oct. 1980: 87.

Rose, Frank. "The Martial Spirit and the Masculine Mystique." Review of *The Lords of Discipline*. *Washington Post Book World* 19 Oct 1980.

Sandomir, Richard. "Recipes for a Novelist's Memoirs." *New York Times*, December 8, 2004.

See, Carolyn. Review of *My Reading Life*. *Washington Post*, November 25, 2010.

Shapiro, Laura. Review of *Beach Music*. *Newsweek*, July 17, 1995, 57.

Sheppard, R. Z. "First-Person Portentous." Review of *Beach Music*. *Time*, June 26, 1995.

Shone, Tom. "You Can Go Home Again. And Again." Review of *Beach Music*. *New York Times Book Review*, July 2, 1995.

Skube, Michael. "Family Friction and New Fiction." *Atlanta Journal-Constitution*, July 2, 1995.

Staggs, Sam. "PW Interviews Pat Conroy." *Publishers Weekly*, September 5, 1985, 85–86.

Toolan, David. "The Unfinished Boy and His Pain: Rescuing the Young Hero with Pat Conroy." *Commonweal,* February 1991, 127–31.

Turrentine, Jeff. "When Life Was a Battle for Honor and Dignity." Review of *My Losing Season. Los Angeles Times,* October 13, 2002.

Weeks, Brigitte. "Pat Conroy: Into the Heart of a Family." Review of *The Prince of Tides. Washington Post Book World,* October 12, 1986.

———. "Where Stories Sizzle." Review of *Beach Music. Washington Post Book World,* July 2, 1995.

White, Robert A. "Pat Conroy's 'Gutter Language': *Prince of Tides* in a Lowcountry High School." *English Journal* 81, no. 4 (1992).

Willistein, Paul. "The Southern Way: Pat Conroy Turns Travail into Triumph." *Allentown, Penn., Morning Call,* January 9, 1992.

York, Lamar. "Pat Conroy's Portrait of the Artist as a Young Southerner." *Southern Literary Journal* 19, no. 2 (1987): 34–46.

INDEX